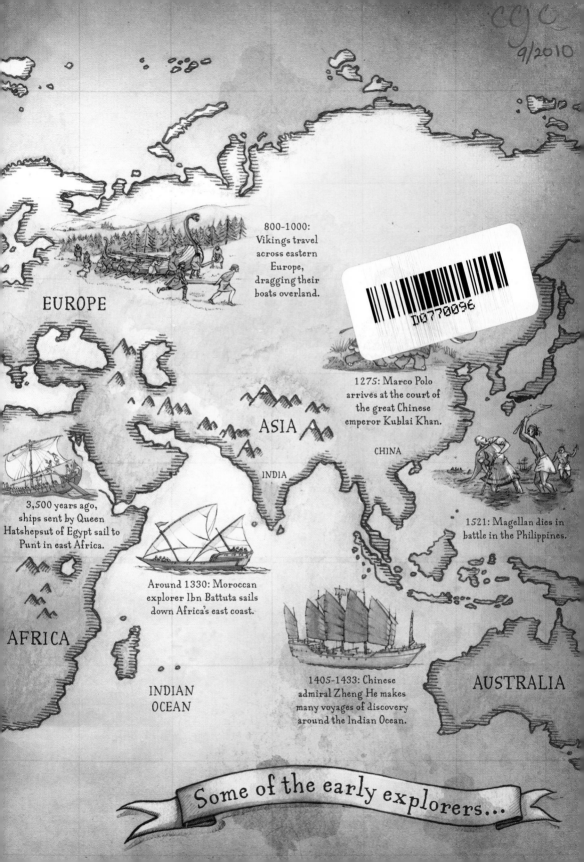

EUROPE

800-1000: Vikings travel across eastern Europe, dragging their boats overland.

1275: Marco Polo arrives at the court of the great Chinese emperor Kublai Khan.

ASIA

CHINA

INDIA

3,500 years ago, ships sent by Queen Hatshepsut of Egypt sail to Punt in east Africa.

1521: Magellan dies in battle in the Philippines.

Around 1330: Moroccan explorer Ibn Battuta sails down Africa's east coast.

AFRICA

INDIAN OCEAN

1405-1433: Chinese admiral Zheng He makes many voyages of discovery around the Indian Ocean.

AUSTRALIA

## Some of the early explorers...

# The Story of Exploration

## Usborne Quicklinks

The Usborne Quicklinks website is packed with thousands of links to all the best websites on the internet. The websites include video clips, sounds, games and animations that support and enhance the information in Usborne internet-linked books. You'll find links to some great sites where you can find out more about amazing journeys of exploration, see pictures, maps and animations, look up all kinds of exploration facts, and even follow today's explorers as they trek to the poles or blast off into space.

To visit the recommended websites for this book, go to the Usborne Quicklinks Website at www.usborne-quicklinks.com and enter the keywords "story of exploration".

The Victoria Falls in southern Africa were named by 19th century explorer David Livingstone, the first European to see them.

# The Story of Exploration

Anna Claybourne

Illustrated by Ian McNee

Designed by Steve Wood

Edited by Jane Chisholm

Consultant: Professor Felipe Fernández-Armesto

Ernest Shackleton's polar exploration
ship *Endurance*, stuck in frozen
sea off the coast of Antarctica

# Contents

This illustrated map made in the 14th century shows Mansa Musa, ruler of the rich kingdom of Mali in West Africa, holding a nugget of gold. This was one of the places Moroccan explorer Ibn Battuta visited on his travels.

# EARLY EXPLORATION

Thousands of years ago – before the invention of cars, trains, planes, or any kind of wheeled vehicles – some intrepid adventurers made extraordinary journeys to distant lands, covering huge distances by boat and on foot. Some went on pilgrimages, or to trade goods, but others went simply to explore and discover new lands and unfamiliar peoples.

This old illustration shows the
pyramids on the edge of the Nile, the
great waterway of Ancient Egypt. It was
used by explorers and traders to travel
south - into what is now Sudan - and
north, into the Mediterranean Sea.

# Ancient adventurers

The first explorers whose adventures we know much about were the Ancient Egyptians. They built up a great civilization over 5,000 years ago, along the fertile banks of the mighty Nile river, which weaves its way from the mountains of East Africa to the Mediterranean Sea.

With the Nile as their main thoroughfare, the Ancient Egyptians became expert seafarers. They had also developed writing, which meant they could record where they'd been and what they'd seen.

## The land of Yam

An Ancient Egyptian adventurer named Harkhuf was probably the first explorer whose story survives in writing. According to inscriptions on his tombstone, the king of Egypt sent Harkhuf on several trips to explore a place called Yam, a land to the south of Egypt.

Harkhuf met Yam's leaders and exchanged gifts. He returned with precious treasures, such as ivory and incense, as well as wild animals and a pygmy dancer to entertain the court. The pygmies were very small people, originally from central Africa, and the Egyptians were curious about them.

## The king's letter

King Pepi II was only around eight years old when he came to the throne. He was thrilled to hear that an explorer named Harkhuf was bringing a pygmy to dance for him. In fact, he believed the soul of the previous king, Neferkare, would be watching too. In a letter to Harkhuf, he said:

*Hurry and bring with you this pygmy whom you brought from the land of the horizon-dwellers... to gladden the heart, to delight the heart of King Neferkare!*

Pepi described Yam as 'the land of the horizon-dwellers' as it was further away than the horizon.

Egyptian kings and queens liked to watch pygmy dancers entertaining them at court.

9

The Egyptian explorers who went to Punt brought back interesting plants and animals to show to their rulers.

→ Harkhuf's route
→ Necho's expedition
→ Hatshepsut's route
→ Pytheas's route

BRITAIN · SCANDINAVIA · EUROPE · FRANCE · RED SEA · Alexandria · EGYPT · YAM · ARABIA · AFRICA · PUNT

## Exploring Africa

The Egyptians were intrigued by the rest of Africa. Around 3,500 years ago, Queen Hatshepsut organized a great expedition to sail down the Red Sea to the land of Punt.

The queen didn't travel herself, but she sent five boats full of sailors to collect perfumed incense for burning, exotic animals and whatever rare treasures they could find. They returned with monkeys, gold, ivory, a precious wood called ebony, and incenses such as frankincense and myrrh.

## Around the continent

Much later, around 2,500 years ago, another Egyptian ruler, Necho II, organized a far longer and – according to some – even more amazing trip, to explore the entire coast of Africa. The explorers headed off down the Red Sea, and three years later returned via the Mediterranean. They had sailed all the way around Africa – a feat that would not be repeated for over 2,000 years.

## Early world maps

At about the same time, several philosophers and historians from Ancient Greece began to create the first maps of the world. Of course, these maps only showed the parts of the world the Greeks knew about: the area around the Mediterranean Sea, as well as some parts of Africa, Europe, Arabia and Asia.

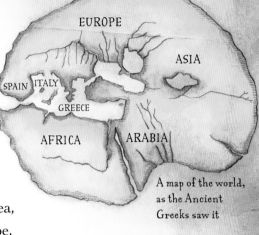

A map of the world, as the Ancient Greeks saw it

## Pytheas heads north

An Ancient Greek explorer named Pytheas sailed across the Mediterranean, past France and north around Britain towards the icy waters of Scandinavia – and back again.

On his travels, he saw sights so astonishing that few people believed his tales. They included amazing light effects known as the northern lights, giant 'fish' as big as boats (which were in fact whales), and vast icebergs floating in the sea.

### Sun at midnight

Greek explorer Pytheas astonished his fellow Greeks when he told them that in the far north he had seen the Sun in the sky in the middle of the night.

He must have reached the Arctic region, where in midsummer the sky is light all night long.

Icebergs like these must have been an extraordinary sight to Pytheas, who came from Greece.

# Viking voyages

HELP! The Vikings are coming! If you lived in Europe between 800 and 1100, that was something you definitely didn't want to hear. Vikings were seafaring warriors, traders and settlers from Scandinavia. People lived in fear of them, because of their reputation for killing, stealing treasure and grabbing valuable land.

## Hats with horns?

Vikings in cartoons often wear metal helmets with horns on them. But there's no evidence real Vikings wore these. They probably wore round helmets with tunics and leggings.

The Vikings' homeland was surrounded by sea, and deep sea inlets called fjords, and they became skilled shipbuilders and seafarers.

## On the move

Many people think of the Vikings as nothing but merciless raiders. It's less well-known that they were amazing explorers too.

As they went in search of trading partners and places to settle, their journeys took them a long, long way from home – to Russia, Arabia, Greenland and even as far as North America.

In fact, the Vikings were among the greatest explorers in history.

GREENLAND

HELLULAND

ICELAND

Viking homelands
in Scandinavia

BALTIC SEA

Orkney Islands

NORTH
AMERICA'S
EAST COAST

MARKLAND

ATLANTIC
OCEAN

SCOTLAND

RUSSIA

L'Anse aux Meadows

IRELAND    York    Lindisfarne

Kiev

VINLAND

ENGLAND    Paris

EUROPE

Rome

Constantinople

Seville

MEDITERRANEAN SEA    Baghdad

NORTH
AFRICA

ARABIA

Viking ships, known as longships,
were small and fast. The earliest ones
were oar-driven, but later models
had sails too.

This map shows some of
the routes the Vikings
took on their travels.

# European adventures

In 793, terrifying dragon-prowed longships
appeared suddenly out of the mist and attacked the
island of Lindisfarne, off the east coast of England.
The Viking raiders grabbed silver and gold from
the island's monastery, and hacked the monks to
death or drowned them. Then they took over parts
of England, Scotland and Ireland.

Viking traders went east as well as
west. Once they'd crossed the
Baltic Sea, they made their way
through eastern Europe and
Russia along a network of rivers.

To get from one river to
the next, the Vikings had
to drag their ships over
the land.

The Vikings decorated objects, like this bronze weather vane, with mythical monsters.

## Boat burials

When wealthy Vikings died, they were often buried in their boats, along with their other possessions. Excavations of boat burials have unearthed Viking jewels, tools and weapons, as well as everyday objects.

A Byzantine king with his scary Varangian bodyguards

## Bodyguards in Byzantium

From Russia, the Vikings ventured south to Arabia and east to Persia (now Iran). But the place they admired most was the fabulous city of Constantinople (now Istanbul, in Turkey), the capital of the empire of Byzantium. With its vast walls, beautiful domed churches and aqueducts, it was famous for its wealth and power.

The Vikings tried to conquer Constantinople, but failed. Instead, they began trading with the city, and worked for the Byzantine emperor as bodyguards. Young Viking men often went to work in Constantinople for a few years as part of their education, before returning to Scandinavia.

## Going beserk!

Vikings – or Varangians, as the Viking guards became known – made excellent bodyguards. Some of them, called 'beserkers' – from *baresark*, a word in the Viking language meaning 'bear-shirt' – could work themselves up into a furious rage, in which they became as fierce as bears and felt no pain.

The Byzantine emperors found this very strange – but also amazingly useful. None of their enemies wanted to mess with a Varangian bodyguard who was going beserk.

14

## American adventures

Viking explorers became the first Europeans ever to set foot in America. Around 980, a Viking named Eric the Red was banished from Iceland as a punishment for murder. He sailed to Greenland and started a settlement there. Once Vikings had settled in Greenland, they must have glimpsed other islands even further west, just off the east coast of North America.

The Skraelings were probably a Native American people called the Beothuck, who had lived in North America for thousands of years.

## Leif's landing

In 1000, Eric the Red's son, Leif Ericsson, set off in search of these islands. He landed in three places, which he named Helluland ('flat rock land'), Markland ('forest land') and Vinland ('vineland') – probably Baffin Island, Labrador, and Newfoundland in what is now Canada.

Leif spent a winter in Vinland, and other Vikings followed him to start settlements. But they got into fights with local Native Americans, who they called 'Skraelings', and eventually sailed back home.

### Remains and ruins

No one was sure the Vikings had reached North America until 1960. Then, the ruins of Viking houses were found at a place called L'Anse aux Meadows in Newfoundland, off Canada's east coast.

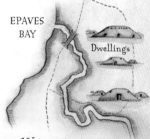

EPAVES BAY

Dwellings

Viking site at L'Anse aux Meadows

These reconstructed huts at L'Anse aux Meadows show what Leif Ericsson's settlement might have looked like.

Turf-topped roofs

# The travels of Marco Polo

**I**n 1298, an Italian sea captain named Marco Polo was languishing in a Genoese jail, after being caught up in a war between the cities of Venice and Genoa. To pass the time, he told his life story to his cellmate, a writer named Rustichello da Pisa, who wrote it down for him. It was the tale of an amazing 24-year journey to China – and the vast deserts, incredible riches and extraordinary sights he had seen along the way. It became a bestseller and it's now famous as *The Travels of Marco Polo*.

## Leaving home

Marco's father, Niccolo, and his uncle Maffeo were merchants who had been as far as Khanbalik (now Beijing) and met the emperor, Kublai Khan. The emperor was curious about Europe, so the Polos agreed to bring some gifts on their next trip. And they decided that 17-year-old Marco could come too. The Polos set off from Venice in 1271, sailing across the Mediterranean Sea to Acre. Then they crossed the desert to the Indian Ocean port of Hormuz, planning to catch a ship to China.

### Asian trading

In the Middle Ages, Europeans imported silk, spices, precious stones and much more from far away in Asia. Goods were carried by land and sea, changing hands at staging posts on the way.

The Polos were among the first merchants to make the whole trip to the Far East.

## Adventure overland

But the ships at Hormuz were floating deathtraps – full of holes and held together with string. So instead they took the Silk Road – a land route across Asia that had been used for centuries by silk traders.

So, sometimes on foot, sometimes on horseback or by camel, the Polos spent three years trekking through harsh, inhospitable desert, scrub and mountains. First, they crossed Persia into the cold, mountainous land of Balashan, which was rich in copper, silver and ruby mines. There, Marco fell sick, and they had to wait a year up in the fresh air of the hills before he recovered.

## Mighty mountains

Once they were on the move again, the Polos crossed the Pamir mountains in central Asia. Marco was sure they must be the highest mountains on Earth. It took weeks to climb them. On their snowy peaks, there were no birds. The air was so thin that even around the campfires it felt mysteriously cold. "However extraordinary it may be thought," he claimed, "fires when lighted do not give the same heat as in lower situations."

### Stopping for a bite

Marco Polo often recalled the local food and drink he tried on his travels – both the delicious and the disgusting. Here are some that he described:

The revolting drinking water at Kierman...

Green as grass, and so nauseous...

...the delicious melons at Sapurgan...

The best melons in the world!

... and the sesame oil at Balashan.

It has more taste than any other.

Marco was right that the Pamirs were very high. Their tallest peak reaches 7,495 m (24,590 ft) – almost as high as Mount Everest.

Some of the things Marco Polo described were too fantastic to be true – like this miraculous stone pillar that stood in mid-air – probably because he hadn't seen them himself.

This map shows Marco Polo's route to Khanbalik in China and back again.

→ Outward journey

--→ Return journey

## Onward and eastward

Beyond the mountains, the Polos journeyed through central Asia to reach China, and saw (or heard tell of) many strange things on the way.

In the great city of Kashkar, they heard about a church with a stone pillar that stood in mid-air without touching the ground. In another city, Marco saw people with big swellings on their legs and necks, which he realized was caused by the water they drank. In another, he was amazed to find women could have more than one husband.

## The desert of Lop

Then they came to the town of Lop, on the edge of the mysterious Desert of Lop (now called the Gobi Desert). There they joined a caravan – a group of herders, traders and animals crossing the desert together for safety. The desert was so dry and barren that no plants or animals could survive there.

EUROPE

Venice

Desert of Lop

Shangdu

BALASHAN

Kashkar

PAMIR MOUNTAINS

Khanbalik

Acre

PERSIA

Jerusalem

Sapurgan

Kierman

Hormuz

CHINA

MEDITERRANEAN SEA

ARABIA

ASIA

Zayton

AFRICA

INDIA

INDIAN OCEAN

SPICE ISLANDS

MADAGASCAR

The locals believed it was full of mischevous spirits that would trick people by calling to them in the voices of their friends and leading them astray. There were strange noises that sounded like singing or drums clashing. But this might have been caused by sand dunes shifting in the wind.

Kublai Khan held power in China from around 1260 until his death in 1294.

## The great Khan

After three years, the Polos reached eastern China, where the great emperor Kublai Khan ruled over a huge empire. First, they visited his summer residence, a beautiful marble palace at Shangdu, or Xanadu. Later, they went with him to his even bigger, newly built palace in Khanbalik, with its intricate carvings, decorations of gold and precious stones, and beautiful gardens.

Marco was astonished by Kublai Khan's incredible wealth. As well as his palaces, he had thousands of servants, trained animals, and treasure stores filled with jewels and gold.

According to Marco Polo's account, Kublai Khan's household included:

- Four chief wives, plus many other wives
- Over 1,000 maidservants
- 12,000 'kasitan', or bodyguards
- 10,000 white horses to provide milk
- Elephants for riding on
- Lions, leopards, lynxes and eagles trained for hunting

### The Mongol empire

Kublai Khan's China was part of a vast area of Asia known as the Mongol empire.

When the Polos visited it in the 1270s, the empire was at its biggest, stretching from the Chinese coast as far west as present-day Turkey and Poland.

It had been created 70 years earlier by Kublai Khan's grandfather, Genghis Khan, who led his armies to conquer other Asian kingdoms. It later broke up into smaller areas.

Marco Polo would
have sailed in a ship like
this – known as a junk
– which you can still see
in Asia today.

# Life in the East

Kublai Khan was thrilled to see Niccolo and Maffeo Polo again, and took an instant liking to young Marco, who was a great storyteller. The Polos stayed for almost 20 years, and Marco visited many parts of the empire that the Khan had never seen, returning to tell him what they were like. In Marco's account of his travels, he described the amazing things he'd encountered. They included all kinds of inventions and ideas that were unknown in Europe at the time.

# Heading home

In 1293, the Khan asked the Polos to escort a princess to marry a Mongol ruler who lived in Persia. They took this chance to make their way home. As friends of the Khan, they no longer had to choose between a long trek and a leaky ship.

The Khan provided a fleet of ships to carry them back to Hormuz. After dropping off the princess, they arrived back in Venice two years later, in 1295.

# Was it all true?

*The Travels of Marco Polo* is still available – you can buy it and read it for yourself. Polo was one of the first Europeans to visit eastern Asia and tell the world what he found there – and his story has inspired generations of explorers ever since. But while Marco was still alive, some people started calling the book 'The Million Lies', as they didn't believe all the extraordinary things in it could possibly be true.

Some of Marco's tales *were* nonsense. He sometimes described things he had only heard about, not seen – such as the claims that in the Spice Islands there were humans with tails, and in Madagascar, there were giant birds that could carry elephants into the sky in their claws.

Nonetheless, experts do believe that most of Marco's account was true.

# A new life at home

Though his far-flung travels were over, Marco Polo's life was not. Once the war with Genoa was finished, he was released from jail, and returned home to Venice, at the age of only 45. He lived to be 70 years old. On his deathbed, a priest asked him if he had really made up his stories.

Marco replied: "I did not tell the half of what I saw, as no one would have believed me." Those were his last words.

## Handwritten hit

Marco Polo's tale first became public in around 1300. But, as printing presses were not invented until about 1450, all the copies had to be written out by hand. This took so long that it was rare for any book to become popular and well-known – but this one did.

Since then, *The Travels of Marco Polo* has been printed millions of times.

# Ibn Battuta's world tour

## The *Dar al-Islam*

In the 1300s, the Muslim world – or *Dar al-Islam*, as it was known – stretched from Europe to China and the Far East.

Ibn Battuta followed two rules to help him travel as far possible.

> 1) Visit as many Muslim countries as possible.
> 2) Never travel the same road twice.

**M**oroccan explorer and lawyer Ibn Battuta is little-known today, but his life was an amazing tale of travel, adventure and escape. He lived over 600 years ago, when there were no planes, trains or even cars to get around. Yet Battuta covered an astonishing 120,000 km (75,000 miles) – equivalent to trekking three times around the world. So how – and why – did he do it?

## A message in a dream

Ibn Battuta was a devout Muslim, a follower of Islam. One of the rules of Islam is that all Muslims should try to visit the holy city of Mecca in Arabia at least once in their lives.

Ibn Battuta first visited Mecca in 1325, when he was 21. While he was there, he dreamed that a huge bird grabbed him in its claws and carried him off to the East. He was told that this dream meant that he would travel to the Muslim lands of the East. Without returning home first, Ibn Battuta set off at once to follow his dream.

22

Here's the tale of what became a 28-year adventure across Europe, Asia and Africa:

## Morocco to Mecca

Even before his dream, Ibn Battuta had come a long way. He'd trekked across Africa from his home, in Tangier in Morocco, to Egypt. He'd sailed up the Nile, hoping to cross the Red Sea to Mecca, but a local war was in the way. So he went overland to Mecca, through the ancient cities of Damascus and Medina. In all, he'd covered 8,000 km (5,000 miles). But Ibn Battuta had barely started.

## Exploring the Il-Khanate

His next move was to cross the Persian Gulf to the Il-Khanate, a large Muslim kingdom that covered a wide area of the Middle East.

The Il-Khanate was home to many poets and scientists, and was full of beautiful old mosques and shrines. Ibn Battuta visited many of the cities, including Basra, Shiraz and Baghdad.

## Powerful friends

While he was there, Ibn Battuta made friends with the Il-Khanate's ruler, Abu Sa'id, and hitched a ride with him to the city of Tabriz. Ibn Battuta soon learned that making friends in high places could help him on his way.

### Lands of learning

From around 800 to 1400, Muslim cities such as Baghdad were home to some of the world's greatest scientists, inventors and mathematicians.

Islamic inventor Al-Jazari built many automatic machines, such as a water-powered robot band, and a water-powered clock with robotic human figures, shown here.

23

Traditional Arabian ships called dhows have been used since Ibn Battuta's time to carry goods and passengers up and down the coast.

## An African expedition

Next, Ibn Battuta sailed along the Red Sea between Africa and Arabia, and on down Africa's east coast, risking attacks by pirates, storms and terrible seasickness. Muslim traders and settlers from Arabia had lived in eastern Africa for centuries, making it part of the Muslim world that Ibn Battuta wanted to explore. He stayed with local Muslim chiefs, and was amazed by the huge, beautiful mosques and gold, ivory and jewels he saw.

### Stinky city

One city Ibn Battuta did *not* like was Zeila. It was the smelliest place he had ever been, thanks to its fish and camel meat trade. He called it:

> The dirtiest, most disagreeable, and most stinking town in the world!

The red lines on this map show Ibn Battuta's routes as he journeyed through the Muslim lands, from North Africa to Europe, Arabia and large parts of Asia.

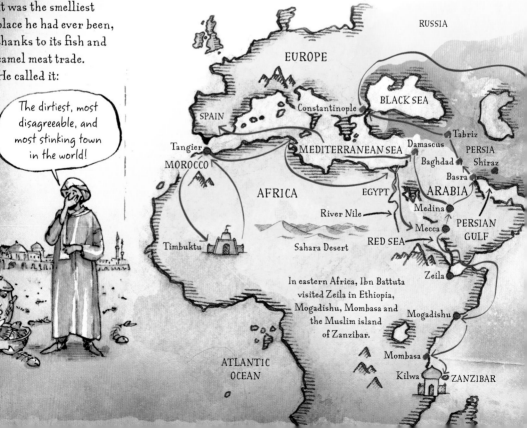

RUSSIA

EUROPE

BLACK SEA

Constantinople

SPAIN

Tangier

MOROCCO

MEDITERRANEAN SEA

Damascus

Tabriz

PERSIA

Baghdad

Shiraz

Basra

AFRICA

EGYPT

ARABIA

River Nile

Medina

PERSIAN GULF

Timbuktu

Sahara Desert

RED SEA

Mecca

Zeila

In eastern Africa, Ibn Battuta visited Zeila in Ethiopia, Mogadishu, Mombasa and the Muslim island of Zanzibar.

Mogadishu

ATLANTIC OCEAN

Mombasa

Kilwa

ZANZIBAR

## A passage to India

Next, Ibn Battuta headed for India. He hoped
to find a job working for its ruler, a powerful
Muslim sultan. From Turkey, he sailed across the
Black Sea to the kingdom of a people known as
the Golden Horde. He made friends with Ozbeg,
the khan (or ruler), who was on his way to India,
and joined his expedition.

After a quick detour to see the sights of
Constantinople, Ibn Battuta finally reached Delhi,
India's capital, in 1334.

The sultan was delighted to see him. He wanted
to encourage the spread of Islam in India, and he
needed lawyers to teach the people the new laws.
He gave Ibn Battuta a job as a *qadi*, or judge. The
plan had worked perfectly.

Or had it...?

> I'll make friends with the sultan (I'm good at that).
> 2) Then I'll ask him for a job (with my skills as a lawyer, he's sure to agree).
> 3) And I'll live in luxury in a royal residence.

Ibn Battuta planned to
find a royal role in India.

### The Hagia Sophia

In Constantinople, Ibn
Battuta saw the Hagia
Sophia, a vast, ancient
building that stands
to this day. Built as a
Christian church in
537, it was already
800 years old when he
arrived. It later became a
Muslim mosque, and is
now a museum.

The Hagia Sophia

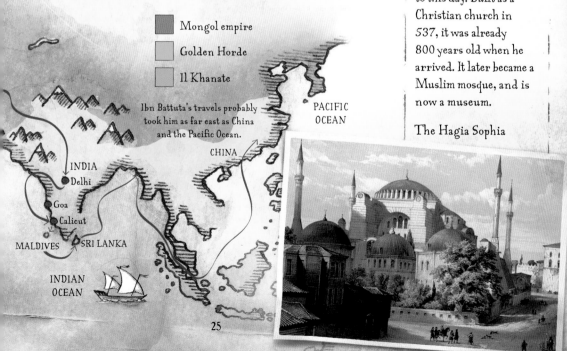

Mongol empire

Golden Horde

Il Khanate

Ibn Battuta's travels probably
took him as far east as China
and the Pacific Ocean.

PACIFIC
OCEAN

CHINA

INDIA
Delhi

Goa
Calicut

MALDIVES    SRI LANKA

INDIAN
OCEAN

Ibn Battuta meets the sultan in his grand court in Delhi.

## A stay with a scary sultan

Unfortunately, Ibn Battuta's new boss was a nightmare. One minute, he would say he was his best friend. The next, he'd fly into a rage and threaten to kill him. And being the sultan's enemy was not a good idea. He handed out horrific punishments to anyone who upset him.

Ibn Battuta survived in India for seven scary years. But when he accidentally befriended one of the sultan's arch-enemies, it was time to leave. The sultan wanted him to go to China as an ambassador, so he grabbed his chance to escape.

### Off with his head!

These are just some of the terrible things that could happen to you if you dared to annoy the scary sultan:

- Being shot from a catapult
- Being cut in half
- Being flayed (skinned) alive
- Having your head cut off and stuck on a pole outside the palace
- Being thrown into a group of elephants with sharp swords fixed to their tusks

## Jinxed journey to China

Ibn Battuta's journey to China went badly from the start. First, he was captured by robbers. He escaped to the coast and caught a ship – but during a stop at Calicut, the ship sailed away, leaving him behind. He found another boat, but when he stopped at the Maldive islands, the people there took him prisoner. When he finally set off again, his ship sank. Another ship rescued him, but that ship was attacked by pirates, and he was washed ashore on the island of Sri Lanka.

Experts aren't sure whether Ibn Battuta actually reached China in the end but, according to his own account, he caught a sailing junk and arrived in China in 1346.

# Home at last

After a tour of China and nearby lands, Ibn Battuta decided it was time to go home. He caught a ship back to India, and made his way through Persia and Arabia. There he found a new horror – the Black Death. Wherever he went, people were dying from this deadly disease. By the time he reached his home city of Tangier in 1349, his own parents had died too.

But Ibn Battuta still had itchy feet. So he set off on one last journey, heading to southern Spain, then on a tour of Morocco itself. Finally, he trekked across the Sahara Desert, and visited the legendary city of Timbuktu, famous for its trade in gold.

# A voyager's tales

When Ibn Battuta finally returned home to Morocco, the sultan there ordered him to tell the story of his amazing adventures to a scribe, so that it could be written down. The result was a book, known as the *Rihla*, which roughly means 'Travels'.

## Timbuktu

Timbuktu is a city in Mali in West Africa, with a long history.

By the mid-1300s it had become a major trading post and a wealthy city, known for its culture and learning. Battuta was one of many explorers who were fascinated by it and made the journey there.

This mud-brick mosque in Timbuktu looks much as it would have done in Battuta's day. The wooden spikes help to support the frame of the building.

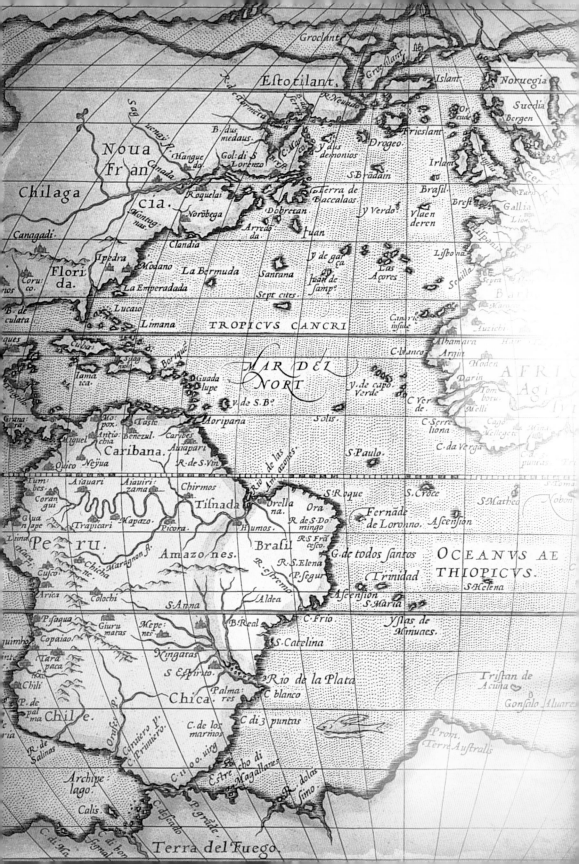

# Opening Up the World

The 1400s ushered in a new age
of exploration, when adventurers
discovered whole new continents,
unknown lands and cultures,
as they journeyed huge distances
in search of trade, treasure
and new territory.

This 16th century map shows the newly
discovered continent of America.
A hundred years earlier, Europeans
didn't know it existed.

This modern Chinese junk is nothing like as big as the 'superjunks' that sailed in Zheng He's fleet .

# Zheng He goes west

In the 15th century, as now, China was one of the richest, most powerful nations on Earth. To show off its strength, the Chinese emperor sent his top admiral Zheng He to travel the world. Among Zheng's goals were to find out as much as he could about other lands – and to make sure everyone knew the Chinese were in charge.

## Who was Zheng He?

Zheng He was born in 1371, into a Muslim family. His father and grandfather had visited the holy city of Mecca in Arabia, thousands of miles away from China, and Zheng grew up hearing fascinating tales of far-flung lands. At the age of 11, he became a servant in the Chinese royal court, serving the great Ming emperor Yongle.

## Seeing the world

Around 1400, Yongle decided to send a fleet of ships to explore what the Chinese called the Western Ocean (now known as the Indian Ocean) – with Zheng He in command.

Over the next 30 years, Zheng led seven expeditions, exploring parts of Arabia, Asia and Africa, and covering more than 50,000 km (30,000 miles). Along the way, he met and befriended the leaders of many other kingdoms.

### The Ming Dynasty

By the 15th century, China was no longer part of the great Mongol empire (see page 19).

It now had a new family, or dynasty, of emperors, known as the Ming Dynasty. They ruled from 1368 to 1644, and were famous for their vast armies and huge building projects.

We have traversed… immense water spaces and have beheld in the ocean huge waves like mountains rising in the sky.

Zheng He

## Making friends

During his seven trips, Zheng pushed further and further west. He sailed south from China, around Southeast Asia as far as India and Arabia, and then down Africa's east coast. Wherever he went, he gave his hosts gifts, such as silk and cooking utensils, and brought back presents for the emperor in return. He brought people too, sent by their countries to visit the Chinese royal court.

### Have a giraffe!

Many of the leaders Zheng met wanted to send gifts to the Chinese emperor as a symbol of friendship. Besides treasures and artworks, they often sent wild animals from their lands, such as ostriches, zebras and giraffes.

## Don't mess with us!

Zheng He's fleet of huge ships, called junks, carried an army of thousands of soldiers, to demonstrate China's power. They rarely had to fight. One look at the vast Chinese fleet, armed to the teeth, sailing in formation, was enough to scare any enemies they might meet. They saw off pirates and sometimes helped local leaders to win battles.

Some of the ships in Zheng's fleet were the biggest boats in the world at the time. Each giant junk had several enormous square sails, and could carry hundreds of people.

The big square sails were made of cloth stiffened with bamboo poles.

Some Chinese junks are thought to have been over 100 m (330 ft) long.

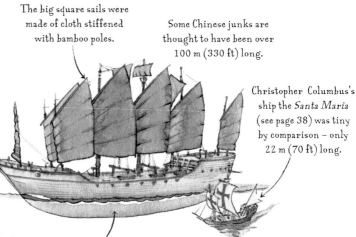

Christopher Columbus's ship the *Santa Maria* (see page 38) was tiny by comparison – only 22 m (70 ft) long.

Junks had a wide, flat bottom, ideal for holding a lot of cargo.

## Mapping the world

Along the way, Zheng He's crews also
made detailed maps and charts of parts of
the Indian Ocean, and records of where
they went. These were to help the
Chinese in future expeditions for trade
and exploration.

But not long after Zheng's last voyage, new
leaders took over in China. They weren't as
interested in travel as Yongle had been, and the
journeys of exploration stopped. Many of Zheng's
maps and records were lost or destroyed.

This copy of one of Zheng
He's original maps
shows the east coast of
India at the top, and the
west coast of Arabia at the
bottom, with the
Persian Gulf in between.

## Watery end

Zheng He was an explorer to the last. In 1433, he
died on the return leg of his final voyage, at 60. He
was buried at sea, off the coast of India.

This map shows the routes of
Zheng He's great voyages.

PERSIAN GULF

ARABIA

AFRICA

INDIA

CHINA

SOUTHEAST ASIA

WESTERN OCEAN

MADAGASCAR

# Around Africa

## Uses for spices

People in the Middle Ages used spices in lots of different ways.

Cloves

Nutmeg

Peppercorns

● Hosts loved to impress guests with spicy banquets, to show off how rich they were.

● Some spices were used as medicines – for example cloves could cure toothaches.

● Spices even featured in 'magic' spells – though, of course, these didn't really work.

In Europe in the Middle Ages, spices were so expensive that you had to be rich to afford them. Pepper, cinnamon, nutmeg and cloves, which we think of as everyday items, were highly prized and hard to find. The reason was that they mostly came from faraway lands in Asia, and the tortuous journey to Europe could take years.

## The spice journey

Spices changed hands many times as they were shipped across the Indian Ocean or carted overland, then taken by sea up across the Mediterranean. Sailing all the way to Asia to pick up the spices would have been much easier and cheaper. But, at that time, no one knew if it was even possible to sail around Africa.

Goods from Asia reached Europe by a complex combination of land and sea transport.

→ Traditional routes

--→ Possible sea route

EUROPE

LAND ROUTE ACROSS ASIA

PORTUGAL

JAPAN

CAPE BOJADOR

AFRICA

ASIA

CHINA

Goa
Calicut INDIA

SPICE ISLANDS

Atlantic Ocean, then known as the 'Green Sea of Darkness'

Malindi

INDIAN OCEAN

If the Portuguese could find a way around Africa, they could sail all the way to the Spice Islands – the name given to islands in Indonesia known for their spices.

CAPE OF STORMS

## Prince Henry's plan

One man who helped
to answer this question
was a Portuguese prince,
often known as Henry the
Navigator. In the 1400s, he
paid for several journeys of
exploration south along the
African coast, in search of new
lands and trading partners.

Now we know what Africa looks like
and how big it is – but no one did then. Henry's
crews charted more and more of the African
coastline, using caravels – small, fast ships with
triangular sails, which could dart along nimbly
and safely. This paved the way for later explorers
to sail all the way around the continent.

EUROPE

AFRICA

ASIA

This map, from 1459,
was as close as people
got to knowing about
the real shape of the
Earth's continents.

## The Green Sea of Darkness

At first, though, Henry's sailors didn't get very far.
They were too scared.

In those days, the Atlantic Ocean
was known as the Green Sea of
Darkness. Its waters were dangerous
and uncharted. For years, no one dared
to sail beyond stormy Cape Bojador on
the African west coast. Seafarers worried
that if they went too far, they would never
find their way back home.

### Sailors' tales
Sailors had all kinds of
scary stories about the
Green Sea of Darkness:

Everyone knows
the Green Sea of
Darkness is beset by
deadly storms!

What if
there are sea
monsters!?

It could even
lead to the end
of the world...
who knows?

35

## Braving the west coast

What Henry needed was someone braver and bolder than your average sailor. Finally he found him. In 1434, Gil Eanes, who had been a servant in Henry's palace, became the first European to sail past Cape Bojador. He didn't go much further, but at least he proved it could be done.

After that, other sailors were willing to follow in his footsteps. Voyage by voyage, they charted more and more of Africa's west coast.

## Cape of Storms

In 1488, Portuguese captain Bartolomeu Dias became the first to sail all the way around the south of Africa into the Indian Ocean.

The seas at the turning point of the southern end of Africa were so rough and wild that Dias named this area the 'Cape of Storms'. But it was soon renamed the 'Cape of Good Hope' – to encourage sailors to keep going all the way to Asia.

### Slave trading

Henry's sailors traded with Africans. They exchanged things like weapons and pans for gold and ivory. But they also took humans back to Portugal as slaves.

Captured Africans were tied together like this to be marched to waiting ships.

Even in the 19th century, when this painting was made, the Cape of Good Hope was a dangerous place for ships to sail.

Vasco da Gama

# A passage to India

So who would be the first to complete the trip, and reach Asia by the new route? That glory fell to a Portuguese nobleman, Vasco da Gama – although, of course, he could never have done it without all the other sailors who had gone before him.

Da Gama left Portugal on July 8, 1497, hoping to sail around Africa, then north to India. It took him four months to reach the Cape of Good Hope. After braving its stormy waters, he found himself sailing up the Indian Ocean, past bustling East African ports run by Arab traders.

From Malindi in East Africa, da Gama followed Arabian trade routes across the Indian Ocean, reaching Calicut, India, on May 20, 1498. He had done it: he had found the sea route to Asia!

After his first visit, Portuguese leaders sent Vasco da Gama to keep doing business with India. He made two more voyages, but on his third trip to India, he died there from malaria.

# Hats and honey

Da Gama had brought a cargo of European hats, honey, washbasins and striped cloth to trade. But the Zamorin, or king, of Calicut was less than impressed. He laughed at da Gama's goods, saying what he really wanted was silver and gold, in exchange for India's precious spices.

But da Gama had still achieved a lot. After sailing back to Portugal the way he had come, he was welcomed as a hero, awarded a salary for life and given a grand title: 'Admiral of the Sea of India'.

### Doing a deal
Vasco da Gama had to agree trading rights and routes with the king of Calicut.

Hmm... you can come back, if you bring something useful!

# Christopher Columbus: the truth

**Man of many names**
'Christopher Columbus' is the English name for Cristoforo Columbo (his real name in Italian). In Portugal, he was known as Cristovão Colon, and in Spain, as Cristobal Colon.

Columbus led an expedition as captain of the *Santa María*, the largest of three ships.

Lots of people have heard of Christopher Columbus, the explorer who discovered America. But the truth is: he didn't. Apart from the Native Americans, the Vikings were there first. Columbus never even set foot on the North American mainland. And, most amazing of all, he didn't even realize where he was. Here is the true story of a little-understood explorer.

## A man with a plan

Columbus was born in Italy in 1451, and went to sea at the age of 14. In 1476, he moved to Portugal, after being shipwrecked there. At that time, the Portuguese were trying to reach the Spice Islands of Asia by sailing around Africa.

But some people had other ideas. What if you sailed west, across the Atlantic? It might be possible to go all the way around the world and reach Japan, China and the rest of Asia the other way.

The *Santa María*

The *Niña*

The *Pinta*

## A flat Earth?

You might have heard that in those days, people thought the Earth was flat. In fact it's not true: most people knew it was round. But what they didn't know was what lay to the west of Europe, or how to navigate these unknown seas.

## Mathematical miscalculation

Columbus calculated that you could reach Japan by sailing 4,800 km (3,000 miles) west. Even in those days, sailing ships could make that distance easily, so he thought it would be a simple journey.

But Columbus's calculations were wrong. He had made the distance too short. And he didn't know that between Europe and Asia lay a vast land mass – the Americas. A few Vikings had sailed there 500 years earlier, but Europeans knew little about this.

## Voyage into the unknown

In 1485, Columbus asked King Joao II of Portugal to pay for an expedition to sail west across the Atlantic, to look for Asia and the Spice Islands. Joao refused. But Spain's rulers, Isabella and Ferdinand, agreed to support the trip, and helped Columbus collect money from bankers and wealthy patrons. And so, on August 3, 1492, Columbus set off from Spain.

It's simple. I'll just sail around the world, and I'll find Asia here!

In fact, North and South America were in the place where Columbus thought he would find Asia.

## All for Spain

Queen Isabella and King Ferdinand of Spain let Columbus sail on their behalf and helped him find money – as long as there was something in it for them.

If you find any new lands or any gold, you must claim them for Spain. If you succeed, we'll reward you well.

Don't worry dear, he'll never come back alive...

Sailors used an instrument called an astrolabe to measure the positions of the Sun and stars and help them navigate.

### The quest for Japan

Columbus wrote many journals and letters about his voyages. After finding land, he said:

I am determined to proceed onward and ascertain whether I can reach Cipango*.

*Cipango was an old name for Japan.

# Voyage 1: Landfall!

Columbus set sail, with a fleet of three ships – the *Santa María*, the *Pinta* and the *Niña* – and a crew of around 90 men. After stopping to repair their ships in the Canary Islands, off the coast of West Africa, they set off across the great Atlantic Ocean.

Weeks went by, and the crew began to panic. They worried that the wind direction would make it almost impossible to get home. Many of them wanted to hurry back to Spain while they still could.

## Land ahoy!

But at last, on October 12, 1492, they spotted land: they had reached one of the islands in the Caribbean Sea. Columbus was thrilled. Thrilled that he had reached Asia, that is. He was sure that he'd sailed past Cipango – what he called Japan – and was nearing China.

## Time to go home

Then, disaster struck – the *Santa María* was wrecked on the island of Hispaniola. Columbus used the wood to build a fort named La Navidad. He left 40 men there, promising to return to pick them up later. The *Niña* and the *Pinta* sailed back to Spain, arriving on March 15, 1493.

# I'm back!

As well as tales of his travels, Columbus brought back wild plants, birds, and gold – the treasure Europeans wanted most. Impressed, Isabella and Ferdinand paid for a new expedition to find more land and riches.

## Voyage 2: Disaster and disappointment

Columbus set off again in September 1493 with 17 ships and over 1,000 crew, including his two brothers. He took horses, cows and sheep too, intending to set up new farms and towns.

But in Hispaniola, Columbus found La Navidad destroyed, and his men murdered. The Spaniards had fallen out with the local Taino people, who had burned the fort to the ground. Columbus sailed along the coast and set up a new town, named Isabela, after the Spanish queen.

Maize, or corn, was one of the plants Columbus brought back to Europe, where it was previously unknown.

### The 'Indians'

There were already people in the Americas when Columbus arrived. As he thought he was in Asia, he called these islands the 'Indies' – a name for eastern lands – and the local 'Indians'. This is why Native Americans were known as Indians.

Voyages of Christopher Columbus

➤ 1st Voyage 1492-93
➤ 2nd Voyage 1493-96
➤ 3rd Voyage 1498-1500
➤ 4th Voyage 1502-04

Columbus set up his settlements on the island of Hispaniola. Today, Hispaniola is divided into two countries: Haiti and the Dominican Republic.

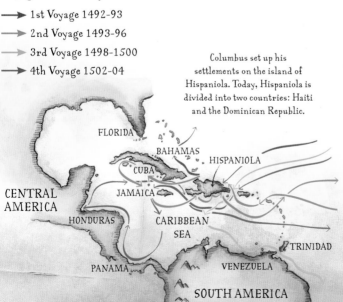

FLORIDA

BAHAMAS

HISPANIOLA

CUBA

JAMAICA

CENTRAL
AMERICA

HONDURAS

CARIBBEAN
SEA

PANAMA

VENEZUELA

TRINIDAD

SOUTH AMERICA

The Taino Native American people lived on Hispaniola when Columbus landed there.

## Now, where's China?

Next, Columbus set off to look for China, which he was sure couldn't be far away. But, to his dismay, he couldn't find it anywhere. He was so embarrassed he made all his men pretend they had seen it. But of course we know now he was nowhere near it.

He stayed in Hispaniola until 1496, then sailed back to Spain, leaving his brothers in charge of the Spanish settlements.

## Voyage 3: From bad to worse

In 1498, the Spaniards sent another six ships across the Atlantic. Three headed for Hispaniola. The other three, commanded by Columbus, went exploring. They discovered Trinidad, and the nearby coast of what is now Venezuela.

But the Spanish settlers in Hispaniola turned against Columbus, furious with the way his brothers were running things. Isabella and Ferdinand sent a new ruler, Francisco de Bobadilla, to take control. Bobadilla arrested Columbus and his brothers, and sent them back to Spain in chains – powerless and humiliated.

### Taking over

When he first arrived, Columbus was friendly with the native people. But the Spaniards soon began to treat the locals badly, taking their land and gold, and making them work as slaves. And many Taino people died from European diseases spread by the explorers. Eventually, Taino society and culture on Hispaniola were destroyed.

## Voyage 4: Wrecked and ruined

You'd think Columbus would have been sick of exploring by now. But, in 1502, after his release from prison, he was off again, with four creaky old ships. This time he wanted to look for the sea channel linking China to the Indian Ocean. But as he wasn't in Asia, he had no hope of finding it.

Instead, he set foot in present-day Honduras and Panama, and found plenty of gold. But one of his ships was attacked, another sank, and the last two fell apart. Columbus had to hire another ship to get home, and finally arrived in Spain in 1504. He'd been unwell for a long time, and he died two years later, at the age of 54.

## The New World

Columbus never stopped claiming that he really had sailed around the world to Asia. But even before his death, other Europeans had begun to realize that the lands Columbus had found were not Asia at all, but a completely new continent.

At first it was just known as 'the New World'. Later, map-makers gave it a name: 'America' after another Italian explorer, Amerigo Vespucci.

In a letter to the king and queen of Spain in 1503, Columbus complained about what a rotten time he was having:

> ... My ships were pierced by borers* more than a honeycomb and the crew entirely frozen with fear and in despair... After eight days, I put to sea again, and reached Jamaica... with three pumps, and the use of pots and kettles, we could scarcely clear the water that came into the ship...
>
> *Shipworm

People eventually realized that the local languages, wildlife and star patterns they saw in the New World didn't match up with what they knew about eastern Asia.

This Caribbean coastline is typical of the places Columbus found on his travels.

You're not Japanese, are you?

No

43

# The conquering conquistadors

## Finders keepers?

Conquistador means 'conqueror' – and that's what conquistadors did. They took over other lands, and claimed them for Spain – and helped themselves to large amounts of treasure too.

In this painting, conquistador Hernán Cortes orders his men to capture an Aztec leader, Guatimocin.

By the beginning of the 1500s, one news story dominated Europe: the discovery of the New World. It was becoming clear that the huge land mass that Christopher Columbus had found was not Asia, but a whole new continent.

No one yet knew how big it was, or what landscapes and riches it might contain. All that was waiting to be discovered by whichever explorers got there first.

## Spain leads the way

Many Spanish noblemen couldn't wait to follow in Columbus's footsteps and explore this new continent. Some merely wanted to settle there, but others were warlike leaders whose object was to invade and grab large areas of land for themselves.

They became known as the conquistadors.

# Early bird: Juan Ponce de León

Juan Ponce de León first saw the New World in 1493, as a sailor on one of Columbus's ships. He became one of the first conquistadors. In 1502, he settled on the Caribbean island of Hispaniola.

## A fierce war and a futile search

From Hispaniola, he sailed to an island called Boriken and became involved in a violent war with the native people. He claimed the island for Spain, and it's now known as Puerto Rico.

Then he went in search of another island, where he'd heard stories of a magical 'Fountain of Youth' that could restore youth to whoever drank from it. Of course he never found it. But he did discover the Gulf Stream current, and a piece of land he thought was an island, which he named Florida. He was the first European to set foot there.

## De Cuellar takes Cuba

Diego Velázquez de Cuellar was also on Columbus's 1493 voyage. In 1511, he led the Spanish conquest of the island of Cuba, and was made its governor, or ruler. Cuba soon became an important Spanish base, and de Cuellar sent many other conquistadors on missions from there to explore the surrounding lands. Turn the page to meet some of them...

## Fantasy fountain

There were tales of a magical 'Fountain of Youth' on one of the Caribbean islands. People imagined a spring or pool that they could bathe in or drink from to obtain everlasting youth.

*I'll stay young forever... lots more time for exploring!*

Diego Velázquez de Cuellar founded the Cuban city of Havana. It's still Cuba's capital today.

Cortés was known for his clever strategies and love of wealth. He famously said: "We Spaniards know a sickness of the heart that only gold can cure."

This is what the Aztec city of Tenochtitlán would have looked like in 1519. The city's population was about 200,000 – making it bigger than any city in Spain at that time.

## Cortés, the cunning conquistador

Hernán Cortés is the most famous conquistador of them all. In 1519, de Cuellar sent him to explore the area that is now Mexico. But Cortés didn't follow orders – he had his own plans.

After landing on the shore, he marched inland, where he'd heard of a huge, wealthy city, rich in gold. It was Tenochtitlán, capital of a powerful empire ruled by a people called the Aztecs.

## Invading army

On the way to Tenochtitlán, cunning Cortés teamed up with local people who hated the Aztec emperor, Montezuma II. His army swelled from a few hundred to several thousand men. Conquering towns along the way, they marched on Tenochtitlán.

Central square with temples and a pyramid for human sacrifices

The priests lived inside the temple square.

The streets were laid out according to a neatly planned grid pattern.

There were workshops and farms around the edge of the lake.

Causeways linked the city to the mainland.

# Who are you?

Built on a group of islands in a lake, the city was even grander than Cortés could ever have imagined, with beautiful temples and treasures. Its people were amazed by the Spaniards' horses, guns and fair skins. According to legend, some of them believed Cortés was their god Quetzalcoatl. They gave him and his men gifts of gold and a palace to stay in.

Quetzalcoatl, from an Aztec painting

# Things get ugly

Soon, however, Cortés locked up Montezuma and took command. Then he went to the coast to fight off an army de Cuellar had sent to arrest him. While he was away, a battle broke out between the Spaniards and the Aztecs, and Montezuma was killed. The Aztecs then drove out the Spaniards.

Stubborn Cortés didn't give up. He gathered a new army and returned a year later. This time he beseiged the city and gradually took it over. By August 1521, he was in control of the Aztec empire.

# Hey! Where's the gold?

But the Aztecs had hidden the city's gold, and Cortés didn't know where it was. He tortured the new emperor, Cuauhtémoc, until he revealed the treasure had been thrown into a canal. Try as he might, Cortés never found it.

## We'll help you!

The Aztecs were very unpopular with other peoples in the area. They demanded food and treasure from them and even used them for human sacrifice rituals. This made it easy for Cortés to gather local armies to fight Montezuma.

Aztec emperor Montezuma

### Francisco Pizarro

Many conquistadors treated the local people very badly. Francisco Pizarro, who conquered Peru (see opposite) was probably the most money-crazed and murderous of them all.

# Cabeza de Vaca

Alvar Nuñez Cabeza de Vaca – whose name means 'head of a cow' – was one of 300 sailors marooned in Florida during a Spanish expedition in 1528. The castaways built their own boats and tried to sail to Cuba. Most of them starved or drowned, but a few reached what is now Texas.

From there, Cabeza de Vaca trekked across North America, along with an African explorer named Estevanico and two other sailors. They met many native peoples as they went, and Cabeza de Vaca wrote a journal about his travels.

The red line shows Cabeza de Vaca's route across America and the Caribbean.

Go on – ask me how I got my name!

One of my ancestors helped a Spanish army win a big battle. He used a cow's skull as a sign to show them a secret route through the mountains. From then on, he was known as 'Head of a Cow' – and it's been our family name ever since.

# A change of heart

Cabeza de Vaca's trip made him realize that the way many conquistadors were behaving was wrong – killing people and stealing just to get rich. He wrote to the Spanish king to ask that the local people be treated with kindness. But it made little difference.

## Power in Peru: Francisco Pizarro

One of the most famous conquistadors, Francisco Pizarro, spent many years sailing up and down the Pacific coast, looting gold from native cities to send back to Spain. Inspired by Cortés's success in Mexico, he headed south, hoping to conquer the rich empire of the Incas in what is now Peru.

When he arrived there, the Inca emperor Atahualpa invited the Spaniards to meet him. Pizarro politely accepted. But as soon as he arrived, the cheating conquistador took his host prisoner.

Atahualpa offered the Spanish a roomful of treasure in return for his freedom. But, once the ransom was paid, Pizarro had the emperor killed. Pizarro founded the city of Lima, now Peru's capital.

## What the conquistadors left behind

Place names all over North and South America show where the Spanish went – from San Francisco to Tierra del Fuego. The invaders brought Spanish-style buildings to the Americas, as well as their language. Today most South and Central Americans are Spanish speakers.

### Amazon adventure

Francisco de Orellana was another conquistador who did more exploring than conquering.

In 1541, he joined a mission to search for cinnamon and gold in the South American jungle. He ended up following the Amazon 4,000 km (2,500 miles) to the Atlantic Ocean.

ATLANTIC OCEAN

De Orellana's route along the Amazon

PERU

SOUTH AMERICA

Lima

PACIFIC OCEAN

A Spanish-style fort in Cuba, built in the days of Spanish control

Magellan's exploration fleet, made up of five ships

# Around the world in 1,080 days

## Mine, all mine!

After the discovery of the New World, Spain helped itself to huge amounts of land and treasure. King Carlos knew that more exploration could mean even more land and riches for him.

**T**oday, you can zoom all the way around the Earth by plane in just two days. But, 500 years ago, no one knew if it was even possible to do it. This is the story of the first ever round-the-world trip, and the man behind it – fearless Ferdinand Magellan. Sadly, Magellan never made it home – but some of his crew completed the journey.

## Inspired by Columbus

In 1493, a 13-year-old Portuguese boy named Ferdinand Magellan made up his mind to become a sailor after hearing about Christopher Columbus's amazing voyage across the Atlantic Ocean. Later, when people realized Columbus had stumbled across a huge new continent – America – Magellan hatched a plan to sail past it and on around the world.

If I sail west, and go **past** the New World, I'll eventually come all the way around to Asia. And I'll claim all the lands I find for Spain!

So, Mr. Magellan – how can I help you? And what's in it for me?

## From Portugal to Spain

Magellan's plans were almost wrecked in 1512, when a leg injury left him with a limp, and he was thrown out of the Portuguese sailing fleet after an argument. But he knew that Spain, Portugal's arch-rival, wanted to find new routes to Asia. So he went to the Spanish king, Carlos I, to ask for help.

## Getting started

King Carlos agreed to pay for the expedition. So Magellan set sail on September 20, 1519, with five ships and around 270 men. They crossed the Atlantic Ocean and sailed down South America's coast, stopping for Christmas Day at the site of modern-day Rio de Janeiro. On December 26, they continued south, searching for a route around or through South America. But where was it? Twice, Magellan thought he'd found it, only to be disappointed.

## Stuck in the south

Winter falls from April to August in the southern hemisphere, and by March 1520, ice and storms were on their way. Magellan stopped at San Julian, in what is now Argentina, until spring. But trouble was brewing. The captains of three of the ships began a mutiny and tried to seize control. Magellan had two of them executed. The other was left behind. That showed the crew who was boss.

### Peculiar Patagonia

Europeans had never visited southern South America before, and Magellan's men saw several things that amazed them:

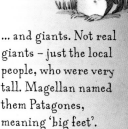

enormous sea lions...

penguins...

... and giants. Not real giants – just the local people, who were very tall. Magellan named them Patagones, meaning 'big feet'.

To this day, southern South America is still called Patagonia, or 'big-foot land'.

51

We've nothing left to eat but leather and sawdust!

Don't forget the rats. The rats are quite tasty.

## Scary scurvy

Scurvy is a horrible disease caused by a lack of Vitamin C, found in fresh fruit and vegetables. Sailors on long journeys often got it when their fresh food ran out.

Scurvy gives you purple skin blotches, nosebleeds and stomach problems, and makes your teeth fall out. If you don't get some Vitamin C pretty soon, it can be deadly.

On long journeys in the Pacific, sailors were always on the lookout for islands, like this one, so they could stock up on water and food.

## Off we go again!

In August, when spring came, Magellan and his men headed south again. On October 21, they found another waterway leading inland. After sailing through it for a month, they caught sight of an ocean on the other side.

One captain, Esteban Gómez, was so scared of this unknown sea, he turned his ship around and fled back to Spain. But the other ships sailed out into the great blue ocean. It was so calm and still, Magellan named it the *Mar Pacifico* – the Pacific, or 'peaceful', Ocean. He thought the Spice Islands of Asia would be just a quick, easy journey away.

## The vast Pacific

But he was terribly wrong. The Pacific is huge. It took three months to cross, and they couldn't find any islands to stop at. The sailors began to develop scurvy and starve, and many died.

At last, on March 6, 1521, around 150 surviving sailors reached the island of Guam, where they found water and food. Ten days later, they came to the islands of the Philippines. Magellan had done it. He had reached the East by sailing west.

## Disaster strikes

But the end was near for Magellan.
In the Philippines, he was caught up
in a battle on the island of Mactan.
On April 27, 1521, he was killed in the
fighting, along with some of his men.

The rest of his crew made for the Spice
Islands, where they stocked up on valuable
spices. Then some of them set off back the way
they had come. But one ship, the *Victoria*, sailed
on, west across the Indian Ocean, around Africa
and back to Spain.

Magellan died in battle
after he agreed to help the
King of the Philippine
island of Cebu fight the
nearby island of Mactan.

The *Victoria* arrived in Spain on September 4,
1522. Just 18 of the original crew were left. They
were the first men in history to have sailed
all the way around the world. It had taken them
1,080 days – or almost three years.

This map shows the
route of the *Victoria*
around the world.

The Strait of Magellan, the
sea route Magellan found at
the tip of South America

# SCIENCE
## AND
# DISCOVERY

T he 1700s in Europe saw the
start of a new age of scientific
study, which gave exploration a new
purpose – to expand the frontiers of
science. Explorers set off to search for
new species of living things, to study
the stars and planets, make better maps,
and chart the world's mountains, ocean
currents, lakes and rivers.

This view of Mount Cajambe, an extinct volcano in
the Andes Mountains, appears in one of the books
written by explorer and naturalist Alexander
Humboldt about his travels in South America.

This black bean flower
is one of hundreds of
botanical paintings
made by Joseph Banks,
a botanist Cook took
with him on his travels.

# The travels of Captain Cook

James Cook is remembered as one of the greatest ocean explorers who ever lived. On three epic voyages, he discovered and named hundreds of coasts and islands, went all the way around the world (twice), and visited the Arctic, the Antarctic, and every ocean and continent in between.

## Cook's early life

Cook was born in 1728 into a poor English farming family, but as he was a bright boy, his father's boss paid for him to go to school. At 16, he moved to Staithes, a seaside village near his home in Norfolk, to work in a grocery store.

But James had other ambitions. He loved hearing tales of adventures from passing sailors, and dreamed of a life at sea. After a year, he asked for a job on board a collier – a coal delivery ship. Later, he worked on merchant ships and on survey ships mapping the coast of Canada.

## The adventure begins

Then, in 1768, the British government asked Cook to lead a scientific expedition to the Pacific Ocean. It was the start of an amazing ten-year career that made Cook a celebrity and put his name on the map – although, in the end, his travels also cost him his life.

### Survey ships

In the 1700s and 1800s, survey ships circled the globe, making maps and charts of coastlines, currents and ocean depths.

This helped both passenger and trading ships to travel more safely, and paved the way for the hi-tech maps we have today.

This portrait of Cook was painted in about 1776, when he had become a famous explorer.

## A transit of Venus

A 'transit' is when a planet passes in front of the Sun. One of Cook's tasks was to measure a transit of Venus, due to take place on June 3, 1769. Tahiti was one of the best places on Earth to see it.

Venus making
a transit

## Antarctica

Of course, the 'Southern Continent' *did* exist – but it's smaller than people expected and is now called Antarctica. It was finally sighted in around 1820, by several different groups of explorers.

# Voyage 1: The South Pacific

Cook set off in 1768 in his ship *Endeavour*. After visiting the island of Tahiti to observe a transit of Venus (see left), he and his crew went in search of the Southern Continent, a huge land people thought lay near the South Pole. They didn't find it, but they did map the coasts of Australia and New Zealand.

# Voyage 2: Another attempt

In 1772, Cook began a new voyage to find the Southern Continent. He sailed so far south, he saw icebergs and ice shelves – but no land. If he had gone just a little further, he would have found Antarctica. Instead, he sailed all the way around it.

Cook mapped more islands in the Pacific, and headed home in July 1775. But he was itching to tackle another mystery – the riddle of the Northwest Passage.

## Voyage 3: The Northwest Passage

The Northwest Passage is a sea route north of Canada, linking the Pacific and Atlantic Oceans. In Cook's time, no one was sure if it existed, so he hoped to find it and chart its coastlines.

In 1777, Cook discovered Hawaii, which made a perfect winter base. In the spring, he headed north and sailed into the Northwest Passage – but ice forced him back to Hawaii for another winter.

## A tragic end

Cook's ships landed in Hawaii during a festival. At first, the people welcomed them, but a fight broke out, and Cook was killed. His crew made their way back to England, arriving in 1780.

### Lono has landed

According to some accounts, when Cook returned to Hawaii in 1779, some Hawaiians thought he was Lono, their god of music and fertility.

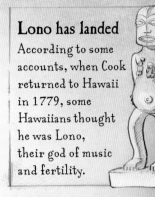

The islands of Hawaii, which Cook called the Sandwich Islands

NIIHAU

KAUAI

OAHU

MOLOKAI

LANAI

MAUI

Cook died here, at Kealakekua Bay, after a fight broke out on the beach.

BIG ISLAND

This old illustration shows the struggle that led to Captain Cook's death, which took place on St. Valentine's day, 1779.

# Cook's journeys

This world map shows the routes of all three of Captain Cook's epic journeys of exploration around the world.

**Key:**
→ Voyage 1  1768-1771
→ Voyage 2  1772-1775
→ Voyage 3  1776-1780

(Cook died February 14, 1779)

Cook was born here, in Marston, Yorkshire, England.

EUROPE

NORTH AMERICA

On all his voyages, Cook sailed south through the Atlantic Ocean to reach the rest of the world.

AFRICA

PACIFIC OCEAN

SOUTH AMERICA

ATLANTIC OCEAN

INDIAN OCEAN

Cook sailed all the way around Antarctica in search of the mysterious Southern Continent.

SOUTHERN OCEAN

Cook's furthest point south

ANTARCTICA

In all, Cook covered a distance of over 200,000 miles, and visited all the world's oceans – and, apart from Antarctica, all of its continents.

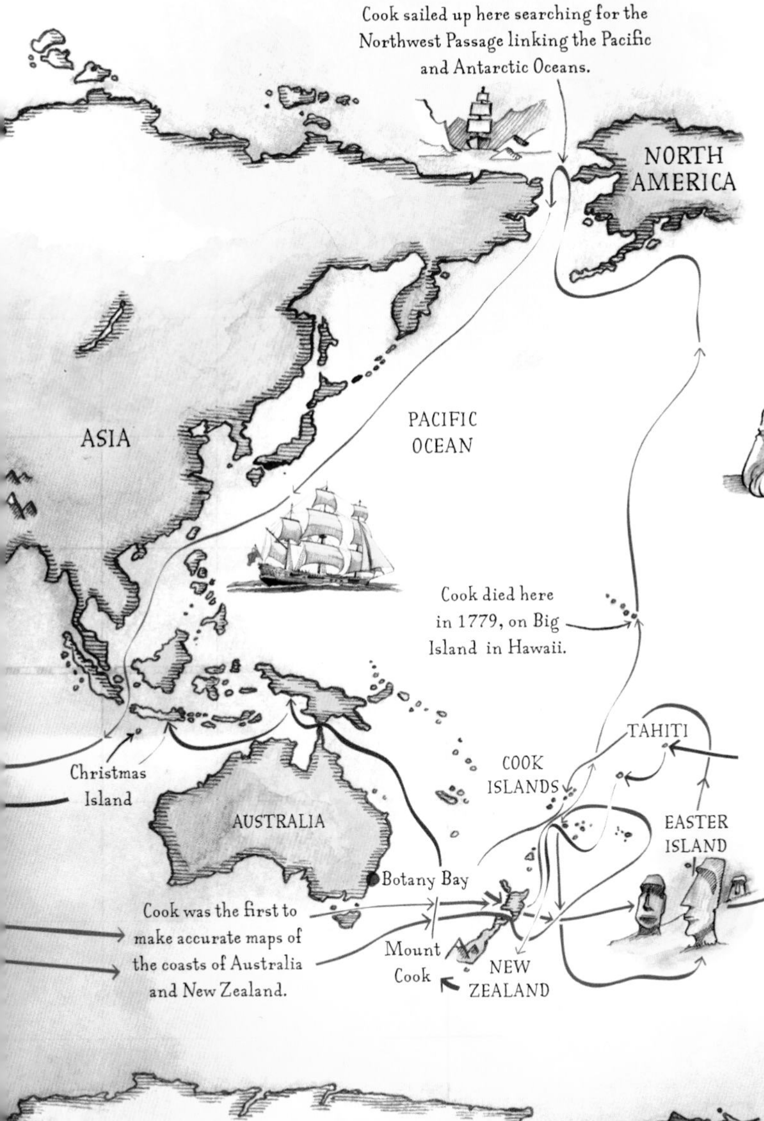

Cook sailed up here searching for the Northwest Passage linking the Pacific and Antarctic Oceans.

NORTH AMERICA

ASIA

PACIFIC OCEAN

Cook died here in 1779, on Big Island in Hawaii.

Christmas Island

TAHITI

COOK ISLANDS

EASTER ISLAND

AUSTRALIA

Botany Bay

Cook was the first to make accurate maps of the coasts of Australia and New Zealand.

Mount Cook

NEW ZEALAND

## Cabbage cure

Cook used a clever trick to make sure the whole crew ate their greens, to help save them from deadly scurvy. He served up pickled cabbage to the senior officers, saying it was a special treat. The rest of the men were jealous and demanded their share.

Hey – he's got more than me!

## Cook's cool clock

Cook used the recently invented chronometer on his voyages – a clock that could tell the time accurately at sea. This let sailors calculate where they were and find out exactly how far they had sailed.

# Humboldt's jungle journey

## Nature lover

As a boy, Humboldt loved collecting natural objects such as acorns, feathers and shells, and sorting them into boxes with carefully written labels.

A s a child in Germany in the 1770s, Alexander von Humboldt was fascinated by nature – rocks, rivers, mountains, weather, the night sky, and all kinds of living things. He longed to be a naturalist and explore the natural world when he grew up.

## Born to explore

As a young man, Humboldt took a 'proper' job as a mine inspector, to please his family. But when his mother died, leaving him a large inheritance, he was free to explore the world.
In 1799, he teamed up with a French botanist, Aimé Bonpland, and set off for South America.

NORTH AMERICA

CUBA

MEXICO

Orinoco River

PACIFIC OCEAN

Rio Casiquiare canal

ATLANTIC OCEAN

Mount Chimborazo

River Amazon

ANDES MOUNTAINS

Lima

SOUTH AMERICA

This map shows Humboldt and Bonpland's routes as they journeyed around South and Central America. Their trip had two main parts.

→ Journey 1 - up the Orinoco River, through steamy rainforest, to study geography, wildlife and local peoples.

→ Journey 2 - along the Andes mountain chain, to look at Inca ruins, volcanoes and sea currents.

# Up the Orinoco

First, the intrepid explorers made their way up the Orinoco River, through thick, steamy jungle. Humboldt had heard tales of a mysterious canal that linked two great rivers, the Orinoco and the Amazon.

Natural canals like this are very rare, and no one knew if this one, known as the Rio Casiquiare, really existed. But after sailing up the Orinoco, through unexplored areas full of fierce crocodiles and biting insects, Humboldt and Bonpland explored the canal and made a map of it.

Humboldt also studied piranhas, fierce river fish with a reputation as deadly killers. But did they really kill people? Humboldt met many locals with piranha-bite scars. The ferocious fish couldn't be that dangerous – or no one would have survived.

## The 'cow tree'

One of the jungle trees was known as the 'cow tree', because it released a white liquid – which was in fact a type of rubber. The locals said you could drink the 'milk', so Humboldt and one of his servants tried it. The servant began to cough up rubber balls!

# Curare cure

Humboldt saw hunters using a plant called curare to make poisoned arrows. Later, a local doctor gave him curare when he became ill and it made him better. Though poisonous, it's a useful medicine in small doses. Humboldt took some back to Europe, and it's still used in medicine to this day.

This is a botanical drawing of a curare flower, which grows on a vine in the South American jungle.

I do not remember ever having received a more dreadful shock...

This is how Humboldt described being shocked by an electric eel.

## Altitude sickness

In the Andes, Humboldt noticed that being very high up could make you feel unwell. He realized that the lack of oxygen at high altitudes could cause a kind of illness, now known as altitude sickness. He also measured the way the air gets colder the higher up you go.

## Ouch! Electric eels!

Humboldt was curious about the electric eels in the Orinoco. The locals caught him some to study, by sending horses into the river to stir them up from the riverbed. Humboldt accidentally stepped on one and got an electric shock.

## Going up!

After sailing to the island of Cuba for a rest, next they headed for the Andes mountains. They climbed several volcanoes including massive Mount Chimborazo, which is 6,310 m (20,700 ft) tall. At the time, it was thought to be the world's highest mountain. Humboldt and Bonpland couldn't reach the summit as it was too steep, but they climbed to over 5,800 m (19,000 ft), breaking the records of their time.

This painting of Mount Chimborazo was made by Humboldt himself.

## Home again

When Humboldt and Bonpland returned to Paris in 1804, thousands turned out to welcome them. They'd been away for five years, and covered an incredible distance – 9,600 km (6,000 miles) all on foot, on horseback, by canoe and by boat.

Having explored rivers, mountains, volcanoes, coastlines and jungles, they brought back with them dozens of trunks packed with more than 60,000 samples of exotic plants, and piles of notebooks and sketches.

Thanks to his daring adventures and fascinating discoveries, Humboldt became a celebrity, had his portrait painted, and dined with royalty.

### Nature notes

The explorers made notes on many plants and animals previously unknown to science. Several species were named after Humboldt, including *Conepatus humboldtii* – Humboldt's hog-nosed skunk.

These illustrations of butterflies are from one of Humboldt's sketchbooks.

## A life of books

But the hard work wasn't over. Humboldt stayed in Paris for another 23 years, working with artists, scientists and museums to produce a series of books and exhibitions to display his discoveries to the public. Then he went back to Germany, where he kept on studying, writing even more books, and giving talks about his amazing adventures.

Humboldt lived to be 90 years old, and when he died he was still working on his final book – all about space and how the universe worked.

Humboldt wrote dozens of books, and over 50,000 letters, describing the things he had seen and his ideas on the natural world.

I haven't finished yet!

# Lewis and Clark's American adventure

## Birth of the USA

The United States of America became an independent nation in 1776, when settlers there broke away from the British, who had ruled them until then.

Thomas Jefferson (see below) helped draft America's Declaration of Independence, and in 1801 became the USA's third president.

In 1803, the United States of America was a lot smaller than it is now. To make it bigger, President Thomas Jefferson bought a huge area of land, west of the Mississippi River, from France. This area of vast plains, deserts and mountains was seen as a wild and savage place, which no one knew much about. So Jefferson asked his secretary, Meriwether Lewis, to go exploring up the Missouri River to its source, and to find a route from there to the Pacific Ocean.

## Lewis and Clark

Lewis picked an old workmate, William Clark, as his second-in-command for the expedition. Lewis, an ex-army captain, was a survival expert and nature-lover. He was brave and clever, but with a terrible temper. Clark was a friendly man, and an experienced soldier and sailor. But he was often unwell, and struggled with writing and spelling, which makes his diaries very hard to read.

## Off we go!

Lewis and Clark built a riverboat for the trip, and chose 33 crewmen. They stocked up on food, clothing, scientific equipment, tools, weapons, and gifts for any Native Americans they might meet along the way.

On May 14, 1804, the expedition set off up the Missouri River from St. Louis, on a 2½-year, 12,000 km (7,000 mile) journey. Here are just a few of the things that happened on the way...

### Well-prepared

Lewis and Clark designed themselves a boat that could be sailed, rowed, pulled by a rope, or punted with long poles.

## Daily dangers

On a typical day, the team would sail, row or drag the boat about 26 km (16 miles) upriver. It was hard work, in sweltering heat, battling biting mosquitoes and dangerous river currents.

They often went ashore to collect nature samples, hunt for food and meet the locals. In the first few months, they befriended many different Native American peoples. A group from the Teton Sioux were less welcoming and a battle almost broke out.

They also took gifts with them, including mirrors, face paint, ribbons, beads, and scissors, to give to local peoples.

Source of the Missouri

Sacagawea joined the expedition here.

Columbia River

North Dakota

ROCKY MOUNTAINS

Missouri River

St. Louis

Mississippi River

PACIFIC OCEAN

THE WEST

ATLANTIC OCEAN

→ Outward journey

--→ Return journey

United States before 1803

New land bought in 1803 (known as 'the Louisiana Purchase')

No! Don't
eat that!

## Native skills

Sacagawea had lots
of useful skills
and knowledge.

● She knew
local languages.

● She helped Lewis and
Clark find their way.

● She knew which plants
were edible and where to
find them.

● She persuaded locals
that the explorers
weren't enemies.

● She saved essential books
when a boat capsized.

Lewis was chased by a
Grizzly bear and had to run
into the river to escape.

Another man got stuck
up a tree when a Grizzly
cornered him.

## Sacagawea joins the crew

About 2,600 km (1,600 miles) up the Missouri,
Lewis and Clark stopped for the winter in what is
now North Dakota. They stayed with the Mandan
and Hidatsa people, and met Charbonneau, a
French trader, and his 16-year-old wife, Sacagawea.
She was a member of the Shoshoni people, but had
been kidnapped by the Hidatsa when she was 12.

Lewis and Clark asked the couple to join their
team, hoping Sacagawea could act as a translator
when they came to Shoshoni lands. She was a huge
help to the expedition, and became one of the
most famous Native Americans in history.

## Bear country

As the river narrowed, the explorers left their
riverboat and continued in smaller boats and
canoes. They came to a high, treeless plain, with
buffaloes, wild sheep and geese to hunt. But there
were also dangerous Grizzly bears that almost
ended up eating Lewis and another
member of the crew.

# Over the mountains

On August 12, the expedition reached the very start of the Missouri, where the river was so narrow they could stand with one foot on each side of it. There they came across the Shoshoni people and Sacagawea immediately recognized the chief, Cameahwait, as her long-lost brother.

Next, with Shoshoni guides, the explorers crossed the freezing Rocky Mountains. There were so few wild animals to hunt, they had to eat three of their horses – and even then, they almost starved. But they were saved by a group of Nez Perce people who gave them some dried fish.

# Paddling to the Pacific

At last, they reached the Columbia River. They built new canoes, and paddled over rocky rapids and waterfalls all the way to the Pacific Ocean.

The following spring, Lewis and Clark began the journey in reverse. In September 1806, they arrived back in St. Louis, where they were welcomed as heroes.

On their return, Lewis and Clark were modest about their successful mission. Lewis wrote a letter to President Jefferson, saying:

*In obedience to your orders we have penetrated the Continent of North America to the Pacific Ocean and sufficiently explored the interior of the country to affirm with confidence that we have discovered the most practicable route which does exist across the continent by means of the navigable branches of the Missouri and Columbia Rivers.*

The explorers killed and ate wild animals such as buffaloes, shown here in this 19th century painting of the plains.

# Dr. Livingstone, I presume?

"**D**r. Livingstone, I presume?" – four of the most famous words in exploration history. But who said them, where and why? And anyway, who was Dr. Livingstone?

## Children at work

In the 19th century, children, like David Livingstone, often worked in factories operating spinning and weaving machines. It was easier for them than adults to climb inside machines to fix broken threads.

It was hard work, but he later said that the experience had given him his great stamina.

## A tough childhood

David Livingstone was born in Scotland, on March 19, 1813. His parents and their seven children lived in a tiny one-room apartment. From the age of 10, David worked in a cotton mill 12 hours a day to help support his family, then stayed up late every night to do his schoolwork.

David had big plans. He hoped to become an explorer and a missionary – someone who tried to spread Christianity in other countries. When he grew up, he studied to be a doctor, so that he could help sick people in the places he visited.

I will go anywhere, provided it is forward.

## Off to Africa

Dr. Robert Moffat, a Scottish missionary who had been working in Africa, met Livingstone and asked if he would like to join him there.

David Livingstone set off for Africa in 1840, when he was 27. He spent the rest of his life there, exploring central and southern Africa, and writing about it. His adventures were to make him one of the most famous explorers ever.

Livingstone described his lion encounter in his book *Missionary Travels in South Africa:*

*Starting, and looking half round, I saw the lion just in the act of springing upon me... Growling horribly close to my ear, he shook me as a terrier dog does a rat... Besides crunching the bone into splinters, he left eleven teeth wounds on the upper part of my arm.*

## Into the desert

Livingstone married Moffat's daughter Mary, and they set up home in Mabotsa in southern Africa. There, Livingstone was attacked by a lion. He survived, but his left arm was never the same again.

But his adventures were far from over. Livingstone wanted to cross the great Kalahari Desert to visit Chief Sebituane, leader of the Makololo people. He set off in 1849 with two friends. They ran out of water and struggled to survive – and didn't find the chief – but they did discover a lake no Europeans had seen before.

## Family misfortunes

Livingstone was so determined to cross the desert that he tried again in 1850. Amazingly, this time, he took his wife and three small children with him. But when two of the children caught a fever, they were all forced to turn back.

### Square or round?

In Mabotsa, Livingstone insisted on building a British-style square house, although local people offered to help him build a traditional round one. He had to make the bricks and fit them together himself.

Traditional village houses in southern Africa are round, like these.

## Saint or snob?

David Livingstone respected Africans and tried to learn their languages and customs. He was horrified by the practice of selling Africans as slaves.

Yet, like many people at the time, he thought European Christians were more civilized than Africans, and that Africans would benefit from being brought under the influence of the British empire.

This waterfall, which Livingstone came across in southern Africa, is one of the world's biggest.

Local people called it *Mosi-oa-Tunya*, meaning 'the smoke that thunders' – Livingstone renamed it Victoria Falls, after the British queen.

# Meeting the chief

Despite his family's suffering, Livingstone still wasn't put off exploring. In 1851, he set off across the desert again. This time, they made it all the way to the land of the Makololo, and were welcomed by Chief Sebituane. Then, Livingstone headed north and discovered the Zambezi River.

After Mary had another baby, Livingstone felt it was safer to send his family back home. His letters and diaries show he missed them terribly, but he believed his work in Africa was more important.

# Trekking across Africa

Livingstone also wanted to set up trade routes for Africans, believing it would help end the cruel slave trade. In 1854, braving terrible fevers, insect bites and threats from local chiefs, he trekked all the way across Africa – from west to east. Back in Britain, news of his travels had made him famous. He met Queen Victoria, received medals, and wrote a best-selling book about his adventures.

## Livingstone's last years

In 1858, Livingstone returned to
Africa with his wife. He made maps
of the Zambezi River, and discovered
Lake Malawi. In 1866, he set out again,
to see where the River Nile began. Instead
he found another vast lake, Lake Tanganyika. But
Livingstone was getting old. After Mary died, he
suffered from tropical illnesses and grief.

For years, no one heard from him.

## A famous meeting

In 1870, the *New York Herald*, a US newspaper,
sent a journalist, Henry Stanley, to look for
Livingstone. After a year searching East Africa,
Stanley tracked him down to the town of Ujiji,
on the shore of Lake Tanganyika, where he found
a pale old man, standing outside a hut. There
was only one person it could be. And so, Stanley
claims, he asked: "Dr. Livingstone, I presume?"

Livingstone was pleased to hear from the outside
world – but he wouldn't leave his beloved Africa.
In 1873, he finally died there.

### Heart of Africa

After Livingstone
died, his African
servants found his
body sitting in a
praying position.

They buried his
heart in Africa, then
took the rest of his
body to the coast to
be shipped back to
Britain, where it now
lies in Westminster
Abbey in London.

Dr. Livingstone,
I presume?

# Mary Kingsley in Africa

Growing up in 1870s England, Mary Kingsley read about Livingstone's travels in Africa. She longed to be an explorer – to travel to mysterious parts of the world that weren't on any map.

## Time to travel

Her chance came when she was 30, and her parents died, leaving her some money. She went to the British Museum and offered to collect wildlife specimens for them in Africa.

In August 1893, Mary sailed to the estuary of Africa's great Congo River. Locals showed her how to make nets from pineapple plants for catching fish. Then she explored the swamps and waterways of the Congo Basin, collecting fish and insect species. Some of the beetles she saw were so big, she said they looked like 'flying lobsters'. She also came face-to-face with huge hippos and hungry crocodiles.

### Jungle gear

For exploring, Mary Kingsley wore a long skirt, petticoats, a hat and a high-collared blouse. She must have been horribly hot, but her outfit was useful. Once, she fell into an animal trap filled with sharp wooden spikes. Her skirts protected her and she was unhurt.

The wild Congo River winds its way through dense jungle.

## Up the Ogooué

Next, Kingsley explored another river, the Ogooué, by steamboat and canoe. She reached remote parts of Africa Europeans had never seen, collecting more wildlife specimens – insects, plants, reptiles, shells, and river fish.

She stayed with the Fang people, studying their culture and religion. Many people feared the Fang, who were said to be cannibals. But Kingsley didn't mind. They taught her how to paddle a river canoe properly, and she traded with them, exchanging British cloth for ivory and rubber. Finally, she climbed 4,095 m (13,435 ft) to the top of Mount Cameroon, the first non-African woman to do so.

Mary was sitting in her canoe on the Ogooué when a crocodile climbed onto it. She later wrote:

*I had to retire to the bows, to keep the balance right, and fetch him a clip on the snout with a paddle, when he withdrew. I should think that crocodile was eight feet long.*

## A dangerous woman

In 1895, Kingsley wrote a book, *Travels in West Africa*, in which she called for Europeans to respect Africans, instead of thinking of them as savages and stealing their land. This annoyed government officials, because Britain was in the process of taking over large parts of Africa. They called her a 'dangerous woman'. But Kingsley was ahead of her time. She saw that all races were equal, and had a right to their own cultures.

In 1899, she set off again – for southern Africa, to collect fish from the Orange River. But she died there of typhoid, in June 1900, at the age of just 37.

This map of Africa shows places Mary Kingsley visited.

AFRICA

Mount Cameroon

Fang People

Ogooué River

Congo River

Orange River

# Across Australia

Australia is a vast continent filled with dry, dusty desert. Dutch sea captain Willem Janszoon was probably the first European to discover it, landing there in 1606.

## The mysterious interior

In the 1780s, after British explorer Captain Cook had mapped the area, Britain took over Australia, and began sending criminals there as a punishment. They and other British settlers gradually built towns along the south and east coasts.

But what lay in the interior? The settlers found large rivers that seemed to flow away from the coast. So some thought there might be a huge lake or inland sea in the heart of the country, into which these rivers flowed.

Some explorers decided to follow the rivers, to see if they could find this spectacular sea. Little did they know what was really waiting for them...

Prisoners were transported to Australia in ships with barred rooms in them, to stop them from escaping.

This photo of the Australian desert shows the kind of landscape explorers such as Burke and Stuart trekked through.

# Outback adventure 1: Sweltering Sturt

In 1828, British army officer Charles Sturt set off to look for the mysterious giant lake. He tried sailing along various rivers, but they always led to other, larger rivers and then back to the sea.

Later, Sturt arranged a new expedition to find Australia's central point. In 1844, he set out from the town of Adelaide with 15 men, into the dry interior or 'Outback'. They soon found out just how inhospitable it was. His men suffered terrible sunburn, heatstroke and scurvy. Food and water shortages made every step exhausting.

But Sturt pressed on. He found water at a creek which he named Cooper's Creek, and a barren wilderness, now known as Sturt's Stony Desert. He almost reached the central point of Australia, but heat and hunger forced him to turn back just 240 km (150 miles) from his goal.

A year and five months after setting out, the team finally made it back to Adelaide, and Sturt received a hero's welcome.

## Outback ordeal

These are just a few of the horrors that faced Sturt and his men...

● Lack of fruit and vegetables gave them scurvy. Black blotches covered their skin, and their gums rotted away.

● Their fingernails cracked and crumbled.

● The heat made lead fall out of pencils!

● It was so hot, their thermometers exploded.

● For a while, Sturt went blind from exhaustion.

Sturt's friend and second-in-command, James Poole, died from scurvy during the trip.

## Native knowledge

The Aborigines (native Australians) often saved explorers' lives. Different groups of Aborigines lived all over Australia, including in the Outback. They knew how to survive the heat, hunt animals, and find water, wild fruit and nuts to eat.

 Burke and Wills

Stuart 1861-62

Giles and Gibson

Outback

Australia's coasts are cooled by the sea and watered by rain, but its interior is mostly a vast, rust-red, scorching hot desert, known as the Outback.

# Outback adventure 2: All the way across

In 1859, Australia's government offered a prize to the first explorer to cross the continent from south to north to find a route for a telegraph cable – and return alive. Two teams took up the challenge. One was led by Irish policeman Robert Burke and his assistant William Wills. Their rival was a Scottish farmer and map-maker, John MacDouall Stuart.

## The race begins

Stuart's team nearly reached the north coast on two separate trips in 1860 and 1861. But thick thorn bushes forced them to turn back.

Meanwhile, Burke, Wills and two others made it to the north coast in 1861. But their food ran low, bad weather slowed them down, and one man died of exhaustion. When they arrived at their base camp at Cooper's Creek, their support team had already given up and left.

## The tables turn

Wandering in the Outback, Burke and Wills both starved to death. Just one of the four, John King, was rescued by Aboriginal people and survived. But he was too late for the prize. John MacDouall Stuart had set off from Adelaide for the third time, following a new route to avoid the thorn bushes. He reached the north coast in July 1862.

Like Charles Sturt before him, Stuart was losing his sight thanks to hunger, heat and the glaring sun, and his men had to carry him in a hammock. But they finally made it back to Adelaide in January 21, 1863, and claimed the prize.

## Outback adventure 3: The wild, wild west

The next challenge was to cross the western desert that lay between the cable route and the Indian Ocean. In 1873, Outback explorer Ernest Giles set out to achieve this with a small team of men.

But things soon went horribly wrong. As Giles was exploring with another man, Alfred Gibson, Gibson's horse died. Giles sent Gibson back to base camp on his own horse to get help. But Gibson was never seen again.

Exhausted and starving, Giles managed to crawl 100 km (60 miles) to safety, surviving on wild foods. After searching for Gibson, Giles named the desert after his missing friend. It's still called the Gibson Desert today.

Burke and Wills tried to survive by eating this plant, nardoo - but it provided hardly any energy.

### Squeaking snack

Ernest Giles managed to catch a young wallaby to eat, which helped him stay alive. He later wrote:

*I heard a faint squeak, and looking about I saw a small wallaby... like an eagle I pounced upon it and ate it, living, raw, dying – fur, skin, bones, skull, and all. The delicious taste of that creature I shall never forget.*

Explorers in the Arctic described
seeing this amazing light show,
now known as the *aurora
borealis*, or northern lights.

# FINAL FRONTIERS

Most of the explorers you've read about so far weren't venturing into completely unknown areas. Although the lands they found were new worlds to them, someone else usually already lived there. But the explorers you're about to meet were truly breaking new ground. They explored the Earth's most hostile and otherworldly places – places so extreme, harsh and strange that people can hardly survive there at all: the icy, freezing cold Poles, and the dark depths of our enormous oceans.

Ernest Shackleton's polar exploration
ship *Endurance*, stuck in the frozen
sea off the coast of Antarctica

# Antarctic adventures

The South Pole, the world's most southerly point, is one of the most remote, inhospitable places on Earth. It's in the middle of Antarctica, a huge, deserted continent that's colder than a freezer, incredibly windy, and full of hazardous mountains and glaciers.

## Shackleton

Antarctica was first discovered around 200 years ago, but it wasn't until 1909 that an explorer ventured close to the South Pole itself. Irish adventurer Ernest Shackleton and his team came within 160 km (100 miles) of it, but had to give up because of bad weather and food shortages.

## The adventure of the *Endurance*

Later, in 1914, Shackleton tried to trek all the way across Antarctica, but his trip went wrong before it even began. His ship, the *Endurance*, was trapped by sea ice, and squeezed so hard that it snapped into splinters. The explorers escaped to nearby Elephant Island in lifeboats.

From there, Shackleton steered a lifeboat 1300 km (800 miles) across stormy seas to another island, South Georgia, to arrange a rescue. It was a close call, but everyone survived – unlike some other polar explorers...

Here's what a famous polar explorer, Robert Falcon Scott, had to say about Antarctica:

Great God! This is an awful place.

Ernest Shackleton described losing his ship to the Antarctic ice:

It was a sickening sensation to feel the decks breaking up under one's feet, the great beams bending and then snapping with a noise like heavy gunfire.

## What are the Poles?

The Poles are the ends of the Earth's axis – the imaginary 'pole' or line that it revolves around. They are the parts of the Earth that are furthest away from the Sun, which is why they are so cold.

North Pole

South Pole

The area around the North Pole is known as the Arctic, and the area around the South Pole is the Antarctic. Around the South Pole lies the continent of Antarctica.

→ Amundsen's route

● Amundsen's base camp (Bay of Whales)

→ Scott's route

● Scott's base camp (Cape Evans)

# The race for the South Pole

After Shackleton failed to reach the South Pole in 1909, another explorer was keen to try. British navy officer Captain Robert Falcon Scott had been to Antarctica before, in 1901. He now planned an expedition all the way to the South Pole to collect Antarctic rock samples. He gathered a crew, and set off in June 1910, in his ship, the *Terra Nova*.

But when he stopped in Australia that October, Scott heard that Norwegian Roald Amundsen was heading for Antarctica in the *Fram*, a ship that had been specially built for polar voyages (see page 89).

## In position

By early 1911, both teams had pressed on through the ice-covered Ross Sea to set up base camps. Scott's was at Cape Evans, near McMurdo Sound. Amundsen's was at the Bay of Whales, slightly closer to the Pole.

The race was on.

Elephant Island

ANTARCTICA

SOUTH POLE

Ross Ice Shelf

Beardmore Glacier

Cape Evans

McMurdo Sound

BAY OF WHALES

ROSS SEA

# Polar preparations

To get to the South Pole, each team had to plan a route, then leave food and fuel supplies along the way. Just a few team members would actually go to the Pole, using up these supplies on their way back.

At their base camp, Scott's men fished in the ice to find fresh food.

But although they had the same basic plan, there were big differences between the two expeditions. They had different equipment, different kinds of food, and different survival strategies:

## CAPTAIN SCOTT'S
### SOUTH POLE SOLUTION

● Base camp is sited on land at Cape Evans, 1,200 km (750 miles) from the South Pole.

● We'll use ponies, motor sleds, and a few sled dogs to lay down supplies along the route. For the final trek to the Pole, we'll pull our own sleds.

● We're packing biscuits made with pure white flour – the best of British!

● There's more to our mission than glory-seeking! Besides being the first to the Pole, we'll collect rock samples for scientists.

● We'll set off as a team of 12 men. On the way, I'll send eight men back, and pick three of the bravest to trek to the Pole with me.

## ROALD AMUNDSEN'S
### ANTARCTIC PLAN

● Base camp is on the Ross Ice Shelf at the Bay of Whales, 1,120 km (700 miles) from the South Pole.

● We'll use small, speedy, lightweight dog sleds to transport everything. If a dog gets injured or worn out, it can be killed and fed to the others.

● Our expedition biscuits have been made from a special healthy recipe, with wholegrain flour, oats and yeast, so they're full of vitamins.

● Forget rock samples! We'll just concentrate on trying to reach the South Pole. That's enough for one expedition!

● A team of eight men will travel to the pole and back, leaving the others at base camp.

## Amundsen powers ahead

Amundsen later recalled how he felt about breaking Shackleton's most southerly record:

*We were further south than... any human being had been... tears forced their way to my eyes.*

Both teams waited until late in the year – when spring reaches the southern hemisphere – to set off. In September 1911, Amundsen made an early start with a team of eight men, but it was dangerously cold. On October 20, he tried again in a team of just five men. Now the weather was better, the Norwegians made great progress. On December 8, they passed Shackleton's furthest point south, just 160 km (100 miles) from the South Pole.

## Scott gets stuck

Scott's team set off on November 1, 1911, but soon ran into problems. The ponies couldn't survive in the snow and ice, and had to be shot. Scott didn't want to use dogs, so the men hauled their sleds themselves, which slowed them down. In mid-December, they were still on the Beardmore Glacier, over 500 km (300 miles) from the Pole.

Dragging heavy sleds like this, Scott and his men could go no faster than around 15 km (9 miles) a day.

# To the Pole!

Scott's team toiled wearily on and finally neared the South Pole. Then, on January 17, 1912, they saw a tent left in the snow. Amundsen had been there first. In fact, he had reached the South Pole over a month earlier, on December 14, 1911.

At the pole itself was another tent. Inside was a letter from Amundsen, asking Scott to take news of his success to the Norwegian king.

While Amundsen's team made it safely back to base camp with their dogs, Scott and his men, miserable and disappointed, were left to drag their sleds home. Blizzards and freezing winds – not to mention the heavy rock samples they were carrying – made progress unbearably slow. They grew weaker and weaker, suffering from frostbite and exhaustion.

...I may be some time

# A sad end

On February 17, one of Scott's men, Edgar Evans, slipped into a coma and died. A month later, another, Captain Oates, walked off into the snow and never came back. Scott and his last two companions, Henry Bowers and Edward Wilson, ended up stuck in their tent, unable to move for cold and hunger, just 18 km (11 miles) from a supply point. By the end of March, they were all dead.

## Dear diary...

Scott kept a diary during his expedition, which was recovered when the tent and bodies were found. Here are some of its last, desperate entries:

*Friday March 16*
Oates... said 'I am just going outside and may be some time.' We have not seen him since.

*Sunday March 18*
My right foot has gone, nearly all the toes...

*Monday March 19*
We have two days' food but barely a day's fuel.

*Thursday March 29*
Every day we have been ready to start for our depot 11 miles away, but outside... it remains a scene of whirling drift. I do not think we can hope for any better things now.

*[Last entry]*
For God's sake look after our people...

Fridtjof Nansen's polar exploration ship, the *Fram*

# Arctic adventures

## Land and sea

The Arctic is the area of sea and land around the North Pole as far as the Arctic Circle. Several countries reach into this, including Norway, Finland, Canada, Russia and Greenland.

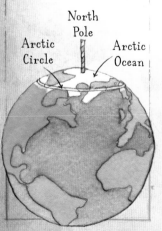

North Pole

Arctic Circle

Arctic Ocean

Unlike the South Pole, the North Pole isn't on land. It's in the Arctic Ocean, where most of the sea is frozen solid all year round. The first explorers reached the Pole using ice-breaking ships and dog sleds. But who got there first?

## The Polaris disaster

In 1871, US explorer Charles Hall set off on an ill-fated attempt to reach the North Pole in the steamship *Polaris*. The ship got trapped in the ice, the crew fought, and Hall himself died after someone on board secretly poisoned his coffee.

The *Polaris* never reached the Pole. It began to sink, and 17 of those on board escaped onto an ice floe. The ship then drifted away and left them stranded. They floated on the ice and caught seals to eat, until a passing ship rescued them.

## The *Fram*

Getting stuck in ice was a problem –
so for his attempt on the North Pole, Norwegian
Fridtjof Nansen built the *Fram* (or 'Forward'), a new
type of ship designed to rise up when squeezed by
ice, instead of being crushed. Setting off from Oslo in
1893, Nansen sailed the *Fram* into the ice, then let it
drift towards the North Pole with the ice floes.

> Suddenly a perfect veil of rays
> showers from the zenith out of the northern
> sky... so fine and bright, like the finest
> of glittering silver threads...

### Northern lights

In the Arctic you
can often see the
northern lights, or
*aurora borealis*.

This pattern of
flickering light in
the sky is caused by
the Earth's magnetic
field drawing in tiny
particles from the
Sun. Fridtjof Nansen
described seeing this
on his North Pole
expedition.

## Nansen heads north

In 1895, Nansen and a companion, Hjalmar
Johansen, left the ship to travel the final stretch
to the Pole by dog sled. They came within 380 km
(240 miles) of the Pole, but dangerous ice forced
them back. They spent the winter on Franz Josef
Land, a group of islands belonging to Russia, until
they were finally rescued by another expedition.

Meanwhile, the crew of the *Fram* returned the
ship safely to Norway, where it was later used by
Roald Amundsen on his trip to Antarctica. Though
Nansen didn't actually reach the North Pole, he is
still admired as one of the greatest explorers ever.

Using husky dogs is one of
the fastest ways to travel
over ice. They can run fast
and keep going for a long
time, and they have warm
coats to keep out the cold.

Arctic Ocean and surrounding land masses with (claimed) routes of:

→ Fridtjof Nansen
→ Robert Peary

ARCTIC CIRCLE

RUSSIA

NORWAY

Franz Josef Land

NORTH POLE

GREENLAND

Peary's base

Ellesmere Island

Mount McKinley

CANADA

## Childhood dream

Robert Peary had dreamed of being the first to the North Pole ever since he had first read about the Arctic, when he was just six years old.

# Peary keeps trying

Robert Peary longed to be the first to the North Pole. He joined the US Navy and went to the Arctic many times. Twice he tried to reach the Pole, but had to turn back because of the cold.

In 1908, at the age of 52, Peary decided to try one last time. His team laid supplies along the route, and on April 2, 1909, Peary, along with his assistant Matthew Henson and four Inuit guides, set off by dog sled for the last leg of the trip. Peary claimed they reached the Pole just four days later.

# I was there first!

But when Peary and Henson went back to the US, another explorer, Dr. Frederick Cook, was stealing their glory. He said he had reached the Pole on April 21, 1908, a year before them, also with Inuit guides and dog sleds.

90

## Who was right?

As it happened, Frederick Cook had also claimed to be the first to climb Mount McKinley, North America's highest mountain, in 1906. But in 1909, another member of that expedition accused him of lying, saying the photos of the summit had been faked. Cook was branded a cheat, and doubt was cast on his polar claims too. So Peary and Henson were finally hailed as the first to the North Pole.

However, some people thought Peary might actually have missed the Pole too. His journey was so quick that he could have miscalculated the distances, and not have reached the Pole at all.

But, finally, in 1989, experts decided he *had* made it there, or at least come very close.

Mount McKinley's highest peak was first scaled in 1913, by Hudson Stuck and Harry Karstens, seven years after Cook's fake claim.

### The winner!

Nowadays, most people agree Peary was the first to the North Pole.

I told you so!

The bathysphere being lowered from a ship to explore underwater

# The deepest depths

## How low can you go?

The deeper you go underwater, the greater the water pressure is. Some sea animals can survive this pressure, but humans can't. The deepest a human has dived unprotected is around 200 m (660ft).

Beebe was thrilled to see strange sea creatures from the bathysphere.

Look at that!

Some whales have bodies that can withstand deep sea water pressure.

At the start of the 20th century, no one had dived deep underwater and lived to tell the tale. People couldn't survive deep ocean water pressure – until a new invention came along...

## The brilliant bathysphere

William Beebe was an animal expert from New York who longed to view the wildlife of the deep oceans. In 1928, he met an engineer, Otis Barton, who had designed a sphere-shaped diving machine, which hung from a cable. They had the machine built and named it the bathysphere (meaning 'deep sphere').

In 1930, Beebe and Barton launched the bathyshere off the coast of Bermuda. Their deepest dive was in August 1934, when the tiny sphere, with both men inside, dangled 923 m (3,028 ft) below the surface of the Atlantic.

## Going deeper

The bathysphere had dived deeper than anyone had dived before – but still nowhere near as deep as the world's deepest oceans.

So Swiss balloonist and inventor Auguste Piccard came up with a new machine that could make even deeper dives. His invention, the bathyscaphe (meaning 'deep boat') didn't hang from a cable. It could move by itself, using an engine for power. As well as a small spherical passenger cabin, similar to the bathysphere, it had large tanks filled with gasoline (which is lighter than water) to help it float, and iron weights to make it sink.

## The deepest dive of all

Piccard developed two bathyscaphes, launching the first in 1947, and the second, named *Trieste*, in 1954. In 1960, the *Trieste* set the all-time record for the deepest dive ever. Carrying Piccard's son Jacques and a US Navy officer, Don Walsh, it journeyed to the deepest point in all the world's oceans. Deeper than Mount Everest is tall, it's in the Pacific Ocean and is called Challenger Deep.

It took over four hours to descend to 10,915 m (35,813 ft). The *Trieste* rested for 20 minutes on the seabed, then headed back to the surface.

Jacques Piccard at the controls of the bathyscaphe *Trieste*

### Deep-sea life

At the time of the *Trieste*'s record dive, experts disagreed about whether living things could survive at the bottom of the deepest oceans.

But as Jacques Piccard and Don Walsh landed on the seabed, Walsh saw a flatfish on the ocean floor. They also spotted a species of shrimp swimming past.

It's alive!

Tropical rainforest in Madagascar, home to many creatures that live nowhere else on Earth. Even today, scientists are discovering new species of animals there.

# More to explore

## Finding a finch

In 2004, scientists discovered a new species of bird – the Yariguies brush finch – in the previously unexplored Yariguies Mountains in Colombia, South America.

Since people began investigating their surroundings, most of the Earth's surface has been explored, described, measured and mapped. But there are still a few mysterious and unknown areas, waiting to be discovered.

## Remote places

Thanks to satellites orbiting the globe, we can take photos of the entire Earth's surface and make accurate maps of it. But there are still some places where no person has ever actually set foot – and others that may be home to native people, but have never been discovered by outsiders. They include some high mountain ranges, especially in icy polar areas, and deep, thick jungles.

## Under the ground

Caves have been investigated since prehistoric times. But they haven't all been explored, as they're often hidden, dangerous or hard to get into. Even now, cavers regularly find new, record-breaking caves, tunnels and underground chambers.

## The vast oceans

The cold, darkness and huge pressure deep underwater means it's difficult and dangerous to explore under the sea. Few submarines are tough enough for the job. Scientists can map the seabed by measuring its depth from the surface – but more than 90% of the ocean floor is still unexplored.

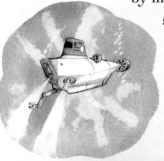

*Alvin*, a small submarine known as a submersible, has taken explorers on many important undersea adventures.

## The final frontier

Even if scientists explored every inch of the planet, there would still be the vast, unexplored expanse of space. In 1961, Yuri Gagarin became the first person in space, and in 1969, astronauts first landed on the Moon. But this is as far as people have been able to travel, so far. There is a whole universe waiting for us.

95

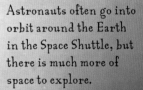

### Depth record

Scientists have long known that the Voronja Cave in Georgia was very deep. But, in 2007, explorers found a new, extra-deep section reaching to 2,191m (7,188 ft) under the ground, making it the deepest cave in the world.

Astronauts often go into orbit around the Earth in the Space Shuttle, but there is much more of space to explore.

# Timeline of exploration

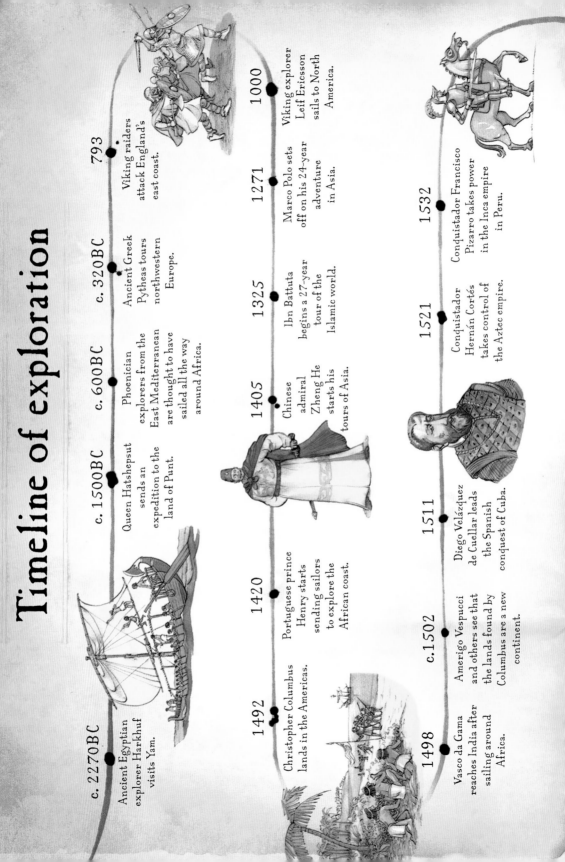

**c. 2270BC**
Ancient Egyptian explorer Harkhuf visits Yam.

**c. 1500BC**
Queen Hatshepsut sends an expedition to the land of Punt.

**c. 600BC**
Phoenician explorers from the East Mediterranean are thought to have sailed all the way around Africa.

**c. 320BC**
Ancient Greek Pytheas tours northwestern Europe.

**793**
Viking raiders attack England's east coast.

**1000**
Viking explorer Leif Ericsson sails to North America.

**1271**
Marco Polo sets off on his 24-year adventure in Asia.

**1325**
Ibn Battuta begins a 27-year tour of the Islamic world.

**1405**
Chinese admiral Zheng He starts his tours of Asia.

**1420**
Portuguese prince Henry starts sending sailors to explore the African coast.

**1492**
Christopher Columbus lands in the Americas.

**1498**
Vasco da Gama reaches India after sailing around Africa.

**c.1502**
Amerigo Vespucci and others see that the lands found by Columbus are a new continent.

**1511**
Diego Velázquez de Cuellar leads the Spanish conquest of Cuba.

**1521**
Conquistador Hernán Cortés takes control of the Aztec empire.

**1532**
Conquistador Francisco Pizarro takes power in the Inca empire in Peru.

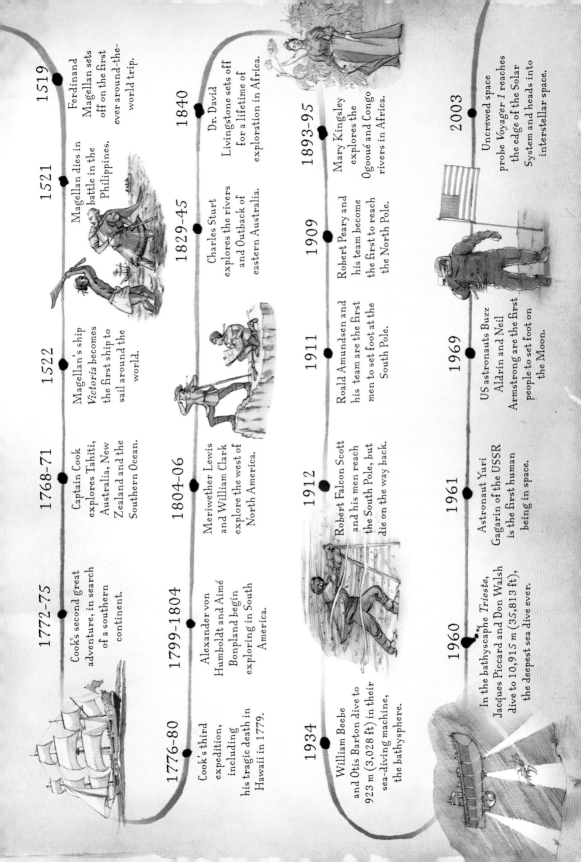

**1519**
Ferdinand Magellan sets off on the first ever around-the-world trip.

**1521**
Magellan dies in battle in the Philippines.

**1522**
Magellan's ship *Victoria* becomes the first ship to sail around the world.

**1768-71**
Captain Cook explores Tahiti, Australia, New Zealand and the Southern Ocean.

**1772-75**
Cook's second great adventure, in search of a southern continent.

**1776-80**
Cook's third expedition, including his tragic death in Hawaii in 1779.

**1799-1804**
Alexander von Humboldt and Aimé Bonpland begin exploring in South America.

**1804-06**
Meriwether Lewis and William Clark explore the west of North America.

**1829-45**
Charles Sturt explores the rivers and Outback of eastern Australia.

**1840**
Dr. David Livingstone sets off for a lifetime of exploration in Africa.

**1893-95**
Mary Kingsley explores the Ogooué and Congo rivers in Africa.

**1909**
Robert Peary and his team become the first to reach the North Pole.

**1911**
Roald Amundsen and his team are the first men to set foot at the South Pole.

**1912**
Robert Falcon Scott and his men reach the South Pole, but die on the way back.

**1934**
William Beebe and Otis Barton dive to 923 m (3,028 ft) in their sea-diving machine, the bathysphere.

**1960**
In the bathyscaphe *Trieste*, Jacques Piccard and Don Walsh dive to 10,915 m (35,813 ft), the deepest sea dive ever.

**1961**
Astronaut Yuri Gagarin of the USSR is the first human being in space.

**1969**
US astronauts Buzz Aldrin and Neil Armstrong are the first people to set foot on the Moon.

**2003**
Uncrewed space probe *Voyager 1* reaches the edge of the Solar System and heads into interstellar space.

# Who's who?

### Roald Amundsen (1872-1928)

Norwegian polar explorer who visited both the Poles. He led the first team to reach the South Pole, arriving there in 1911.

### Abu Abdullah Muhammad Ibn Battuta (c.1304-1369)

This Moroccan adventurer set out to to visit all the world's Muslim lands. He toured much of Arabia and Asia and parts of Africa and Europe.

### William Beebe (1877-1962)

US zoologist, writer and deep-sea explorer who, along with Otis Barton, broke the record for deep-sea diving in 1934, using a purpose-built diving vessel called the bathysphere.

### William Clark (1770-1838)

American soldier and politician. With Meriwether Lewis, he trekked across North America to the Pacific Ocean and back, from 1803-1805.

### Christopher Columbus (1451-1506)

Italian-born sailor and explorer who sailed west across the Atlantic on behalf of Spain in 1492. He was hoping to sail around the world, but instead found the Americas.

### James Cook (1728-1779)

Better known as Captain Cook, this British explorer led three worldwide expeditions to chart coastlines, collect scientific data and search for the land mass later named Antarctica.

### Hernán Cortés (1485-1547)

The most famous of the Spanish conquistadors who took over large parts of the Americas in the 1500s, Cortés is best-known for conquering the land of the Aztecs in what is now Mexico.

### Leif Ericsson (c.970-c.1010)

Viking explorer who sailed West from Greenland to discover parts of the North American mainland around the year 1000.

### Vasco da Gama (c.1460-1524)

Portuguese explorer who, in 1498, became the first to sail eastward around Africa, from Europe to India.

### Alexander von Humboldt (1769-1859)

German scientist, explorer and writer. From 1799-1804, with botanist Aimé Bonpland, he made many important scientific and geographical discoveries in South and Central America

## Mary Kingsley (1862-1900)

English explorer and writer who explored African rivers, collecting plant and animal specimens. She also studied and wrote about local cultures.

## Meriwether Lewis (1774-1809)

American explorer and soldier who, along with William Clark, led the famous 1803-1805 'Lewis and Clark' expedition across North America.

## David Livingstone (1813-1873)

British doctor, missionary and explorer who went to live in Africa and spent his life exploring it and writing about it. He was the first outsider to see many of Africa's great lakes.

## Ferdinand Magellan (c.1480-1521)

Portuguese explorer who led the first expedition to sail all the way around the world, from 1519-1522. Magellan himself, though, died during the trip.

## Robert Peary (1856-1920)

US polar explorer. He led the expedition that is thought to have been the first to reach the North Pole, in 1909.

## Francisco Pizarro (c.1471-1541)

Spanish conquistador, or conqueror, who invaded and took over the Inca empire, in what is now Peru, in the 1530s.

## Marco Polo (c.1254-1324)

Famous Italian explorer who, along with his father and uncle, trekked across Asia from Europe to China. From there, he also visited many other Asian lands.

## Robert Falcon Scott (1868-1912)

British Antarctic explorer who led an expedition to the South Pole, arriving there in 1912. Scott found he had been beaten to the Pole by Roald Amundsen, and he and his team died on their way back.

## John McDouall Stuart (1815-1866)

British-born Stuart became one of the most famous explorers of Australia. In 1862, he led the first expedition to cross Australia from South to North and return safely.

## Charles Sturt (1795-1869)

British explorer famous for his expeditions into the interior of Australia, exploring the Outback and several of Australia's great rivers, in the 1800s.

## Zheng He (1371-1433)

Chinese admiral who captained seven huge sailing expeditions to explore the lands around the Indian Ocean in the 1400s.

# Glossary

**altitude sickness** An illness caused by the low air pressure in high-up places.

**ambassador** Someone who goes abroad as a representative of their country.

**Arctic Circle** An imaginary line around the Arctic, the area around the North Pole.

**astrolabe** Instrument used to measure the height of the Sun or stars above the horizon.

**axis** An imaginary line through the Earth from North to South, which it spins around.

**Aztecs** Native people living in the area that is now Mexico in the 1500s.

**Black Death** A deadly disease, also known as the Plague, that killed millions in the Middle Ages.

**botanist** A scientist who studies plants.

**caravel** A small, light sailing ship with two or three masts.

**chronometer** A very accurate clock designed for keeping good time at sea.

**conquistadors** Spanish invaders who took over large parts of South America and the Caribbean in the 1500s.

**continents** The Earth's large land masses, such as Asia or Africa.

**curare** A very poisonous substance from a plant, which can also be used as a medicine.

**current** A flow of water within a sea or river.

**dhow** A traditional Arabic sailing boat or ship with triangular sails.

**dynasty** A family of rulers in which power is handed on down the generations.

**edible** Good or safe to eat.

**empire** A large area of many lands or kingdoms ruled over by a single power.

**epic** Very long-lasting, impressive or heroic.

**fjord** A deep, long sea inlet formed by glaciers flowing downhill.

**fleet** A group of ships sailing together.

**glacier** A river of compacted snow and ice that moves slowly downhill.

**Gulf Stream** A powerful ocean current that flows up the east coast of North America and across the Atlantic to Europe.

**iceberg** A huge floating chunk of ice that has broken off from a glacier or ice shelf.

**ice floe** A flat section of floating sea ice.

**ice shelf** A thick platform of ice that forms where a glacier pushes out over the sea.

**incense** A substance that is burned to release a scent.

**Indies** An old name for the islands of the Caribbean, used because they were once thought to be part of Asia.

**ivory** A hard, off-white substance that comes from elephants' tusks.

**junk** A traditional Chinese sailing ship with square sails.

**longship** A long, narrow Viking ship powered by sails and oars.

**loot** To steal treasure or other valuables.

**malaria** A dangerous disease spread by mosquito bites.

**merchant** Someone who sells, transports or trades in goods.

**missionary** Someone who travels to try to spread their religion to other people.

**mutiny** An uprising, especially on board a ship, in which the crew members rebel against the captain and try to take over.

**native** Belonging to or coming from a particular place.

**naturalist** Someone who studies nature and wildlife.

**northern lights** A pattern of glowing lights in the sky around the North Pole.

**Northwest Passage** A sea route around the North of Canada, connecting the Pacific and Atlantic Oceans.

**orbit** The path of an object in space, such as a spacecraft or a moon, as it moves around another object, such as a planet.

**Outback** The hot, remote desert or scrub interior of Australia.

**pilgrimage** A journey made to visit a religious shrine or holy place.

**poles** The coldest parts of the Earth, which are furthest away from the Sun.

**prehistoric** From the time before history began to be written down.

**ransom** Money demanded for the release of a hostage or prisoner.

**satellite** A spacecraft in orbit around a planet or other space object.

**scribe** Someone who writes books by hand.

**scurvy** A serious disease caused by a lack of Vitamin C, which is found in fresh fruit and vegetables.

**settlement** A new village, town or city set up by people who have arrived from somewhere else.

**settler** Someone who travels to another place in order to start living there.

**shipworm** A type of tiny sea creature that tunnels holes in wooden ships.

**Silk Road** An ancient trade route across Asia, linking China with Persia and Arabia.

**slave** Someone who is forced to work for someone else for little or no pay.

**space probe** A spacecraft that goes to explore space with no crew on board.

**species** A particular type of living thing.

**strait** A narrow sea channel between two pieces of land.

**typhoid** A deadly disease spread by germs in dirty water or food.

**Vikings** Seafaring people from Scandinavia who explored, raided and settled around Europe from 800-1100.

**wallaby** A small kangaroo-like animal.

# Index

# Acknowledgements

Every effort has been made to trace and acknowledge ownership of copyright. If any rights have been omitted, the publishers offer to rectify this in any future editions following notification. The publishers are grateful to the following individuals and organizations for their permission to reproduce material on the following pages: (t=top, b=bottom, l=left, r=right)

Cover (main) © Bettmann/Corbis; p2-3 © Chad Ehlers/Getty Images; p4-5 © Royal Geographical Society / Alamy; p6 © The Art Archive\JohnWebb; p8 © Time & Life Pictures/Getty Images; p10-11 © Jeremy Walker/ naturepl.com; p12 (b) © Kennan Ward/Corbis; p14 (tl) © Ronald Sheridan@Ancient Art & Architecture Collection Ltd.; p15 (b) © Greg Probst/CORBIS; p16-17 © blickwinkel / Alamy; p20 (b) © SCPhotos / Alamy; p23 (br) © The Metropolitan Museum of Art; p25 (br) Stapleton Collection, UK / The Bridgeman Art Library; p27 (b) © John Elk III / Alamy; p30 © Horizon International Images Limited / Alamy; p35 (tr) Palazzo Ducale, Venice, Italy / Alinari / The Bridgeman Art Library; p36 (b) 'Gale off the Cape of Good Hope' by Thomas Daniell © National Maritime Museum; p37 (tr) British Library, London, UK / The Bridgeman Art Library; p38 (b) Private Collection / Index / The Bridgeman Art Library; p40 (tl) © MICHAEL HOLFORD; p42-43 © Peter Adams/zefa/Corbis; p44 (b) Museo de Bellas Artes, Zaragoza, Spain / The Bridgeman Art Library; p47 (tr) Biblioteca Nazionale Centrale, Florence, Italy / The Bridgeman Art Library; p49 (b) © Ira Block/Getty Images; p50 (t) © North Wind Picture Archives / Alamy; p52 (b) © Eric Nathan / Alamy; p54-55 Bibliotheque Nationale, Paris, France / Giraudon / The Bridgeman Art Library; p56 © Tim Beaglehole, photo Courtesy, New Zealand Electronic Text Centre (http://www.nzetc.org); p57 (br) © The Print Collector / Alamy; p58-59 Private Collection / Photo © Christie's Images / The Bridgeman Art Library; p61 (br) K1 Marine Timekeeper by Larcum Kendall © National Maritime Museum; p63 (br) Mary Evans Picture Library; p64 (b)Private Collection / The Stapleton Collection / The Bridgeman Art Library; p65 (t) Humboldt-Universitaet, Berlin, Germany / © Humboldt-Universitaet zu Berlin / The Bridgeman Art Library; p68-69 Private Collection / Photo © Christie's Images / The Bridgeman Art Library; p71 (b) © Images of Africa Photobank / Alamy; p72 (b) © Panoramic Images/Getty Images; p74 (b) © Kim Gjerstad/Greenpeace; p76-77 © Doug Pearson/JAI/Corbis; p80-81 © Alexander Gabrysch / Alamy; p82 © Hulton-Deutsch Collection/CORBIS; p86 (b) © Hulton-Deutsch Collection/CORBIS; p88 (t) Private Collection / © Look and Learn / The Bridgeman Art Library; p91 (b) © Corbis Premium RF / Alamy; p92 (t) © Illustrated London News Ltd/Mary Evans; p93 (tr) © Bettmann/CORBIS; p94 (t) © Keren Su/China Span / Alamy; p95 (br) © Mark M. Lawrence/CORBIS;

Picture research by Ruth King

First published in 2008 by Usborne Publishing Ltd., Usborne House, 83-85 Saffron Hill, London EC1N 8RT, England. www.usborne.com Copyright © 2009 Usborne Publishing Ltd. The name Usborne and the devices♀⊕ are Trade Marks of Usborne Publishing Ltd.